JUNO THE BAKERY

CRAFTED IN COPENHAGEN

EMIL GLASER
NINA SCHMIEGELOW
WITH NOAH ERHUN

ACKNOWLEDGMENTS

This book is the result of the contributions of everyone who has shared our journey thus far on our continued quest for great craftmanship at Juno the Bakery.

The goal for us with this book has always been to reflect the standards set by the team at Juno the Bakery. This book would not have been possible without the special efforts of Noah Erhun, Matthew Walker and Emily Timmins.

To the whole team, which every day makes the heart at the bakery beat. The greatest thank you.

Several people have been deeply involved in the development of the bakery, notably Arnaud Brun, Noah Erhun, Matthew Walker, Emily Timmins, Maria Luisa Tammaro, Ida Svarrer Dahl, Grace Binnie and Cecilie Høj.

An essential part of this book is of course the collected photos. Thank you, Petra Kleis, for not only taking portrait-like photos of our breads and pastries but also capturing those moments that define the ambience at the bakery. We could easily make another book with just the photos that we couldn't fit into this book.

A special thank you to Jacob Birch for putting all of the pieces together, understanding our thoughts and giving them form.

Thank you to the team at Strandberg Publishing, for showing the utmost professionalism throughout the production, a good portion of patience and support in making this book.

Lastly, thank you to our three sons and our family, whose support from the very first day has been invaluable.

Emil and Nina

PORTRA 800-2
54
M ---- 1/350
AEOver A
603

IMAGINE
THE SCENT OF FRESHLY BAKED
SOURDOUGH BREAD,
FRESHLY GROUND CARDAMOM,
FRESHLY BREWED COFFEE,
SUGAR SLOWLY CARAMELISING AND
THE AROMA OF MELTED BUTTER.
IMAGINE A TEAM DEDICATED TO
ITS ARTISANAL CRAFT, LEARNING,
BAKING, SERVING.
IMAGINE PEOPLE EATING, TALKING,
SHARING.
THIS IS
JUNO THE BAKERY

CONTENTS

A warm cardamom bun on a cold winter day in Stockholm is a culinary memory from my childhood that has stayed with me. Caramelised sugar sticking to my fingers, the soft, sweet dough and the comforting aroma of freshly ground cardamom tickling my nose. Comfort encapsulated. Perhaps this memory unknowingly shifted my path from Michelin-starred kitchens to the world of baking.

I grew up in a small suburb north of Stockholm together with my parents and my little sister in a loving home with great enthusiasm for food. Neither of my parents had any background in cooking, but they cherished a good meal and would travel far to visit a good bakery or shop for specific groceries. They taught me the importance of good ingredients and how simple cooking could be when you source them well. Sitting at the table together and sharing a good meal was inevitable in my home. It was an essential part of the day we always looked forward to and is one of the many things I continue to cherish now with my own children. I particularly remember the weekends, when my mother in the afternoon would line up butter cookies or a cake she had made, and me indulging in her baked goods with a glass of cold milk. My mom loved baking, and she loved books. Spending time in her library, flicking through the hundreds of cookery and baking books she had collected over time could keep me occupied for hours already from my youngest days. I miss her dearly. Knowing that she got to see the beginning of the bakery, how happy she was visiting, and remembering her smile when taking a piece of a newly baked pastry fills me with warmth and meaning.

My parents' love for food initiated the deep love for food I possess today and together with my genuine curiosity, eventually inspiring me to pursue a career within the hospitality industry. A world of flavour, culture and incredible people. Working in some of the best restaurants across the world, from Copenhagen to Tokyo, Monaco and Paris, emphasised that when it comes to creating truly great food everything begins with the quality of the ingredients, and this philosophy is something we have taken with us to the bakery.

After years of working in restaurants I felt it was time for a new challenge: To dive deep into a new area within the world of food. For some time, I had thought about working at a bakery, learning more about bread and pastries. I shared my thoughts with Nina, my beloved wife and business partner. I can't remember why, since we had never baked bread at a large scale nor had operated a company, but it didn't take long until we concluded that we could just open our own bakery. With Nina's background in finance and mine in the kitchen, we had the tools to get started. Most of all, we had a relentless desire to do something exceptional together.

It all began with the idea of creating a neighbourhood bakery, a place we ourselves longed to have on our own street, while living in Paris. A bakery with a small selection of bread and pastries, where everything was freshly baked all day long. Uncompromising and timeless. A bakery that could reflect our Scandinavian heritage and act as a waterhole for the otherwise bustling daily rhythm of the city. Baked goods made with the best ingredients possible and the aspiration of pure flavours and expressions with a recognisable and nostalgic touch. Whether classic or something new.

On December 1st 2017, we opened the doors for the very first time at Århusgade 48. With only 30m^2 everything happened in full openness and so the guests could participate in the action firsthand, from mixing of the dough to rolling of our cardamom buns and selecting pastries straight out of the oven. Often the bakery reminds me of a Beethoven concerto – energetic, emotional, sometimes a bit chaotic but well-orchestrated. I love that feeling.

– Emil Glaser

EQUIPMENT

The recommended equipment will help you achieve a good result and consistency with our recipes. The following are strong suggestions, however it is always possible to use even more basic tools and still succeed – when mixing by hand, for example, or adjusting to differences in the size of cake moulds or tart tins or adapting to the oven that you have. Adjusting the recipes to what you have on hand is all part of the journey.

ESSENTIALS

Stand mixer
A high-quality stand mixer with a 4–6lt bowl will be very helpful for mixing all the sweet doughs that require longer mixing times to be fully developed. A KitchenAid Artisan or Professional with a 4lt or 6lt bowl or other brands with sturdy motors for mixing stiff dough are recommended. Make sure to have a dough hook, paddle and balloon whisk attachment.

Immersion blender
Useful for preparing pastry fillings and ganaches.

Food processor
Frequently used for grinding nuts and making pralines.

Mixing bowls
Range of sizes of stainless steel mixing bowls for scaling and preparing mixes.

Digital scales, 1g sensitivity

A key to consistent baking is a good quality gram scale. We recommend gram measurements for the majority of recipes to improve accuracy.

Digital thermometer, 0–200°C / 32–392°F range. Thermapen is recommended.

Awareness of temperature is a critical starting point for bread as well as chocolate tempering, pastry and lamination. A good quality digital thermometer will provide the ability to respond to changes and help you make adjustments to achieve the desired results. Our daily routines are constantly varied based on ambient and ingredient temperatures, combined with the taste, touch and gut feeling that come with repetition.

Dough scrapers
A large metal or plastic dough scraper, about 15cm / 6in wide for shaping bread and dividing sourdough buns will be very helpful.

Pastry cards
A few smaller soft plastic pastry cards for scraping down the mixing bowl, transferring batters and filling piping bags.

Rolling pin
A cornerstone of our baking style is a sturdy, heavy rolling pin, helping us to smoothly apply even pressure to the soft bun doughs that we work with. Especially for producing laminated pastries at home a good rolling pin will be essential.

Dowel rolling pin
A 45cm / 18in long wood or metal dowel, 2.5cm / 1in diameter without tapering, will be used for dividing bun doughs and laminated products.

Pizza cutter
One of the most used tools in the bakery is a sturdy pizza cutter for dividing all of the sweet doughs.

Spiked docking roller
To prevent air bubbles and for an even rise we use the docking roller for our sablés and flat breads.

Large offset palette knife, 15–20cm / 6–8in

For neatly and evenly spreading fillings and cake batters a palette knife is what works best for us.

Baking trays
Heavy baking trays with good heat transfer are important for the even baking of most products.

Cake and rye bread tins
Perfect for both cakes and bread baking, we use thick-walled metal baking tins, 10cm deep, 10cm wide, 18cm long / 4 × 4 × 7in.

Pastry brush
A 4–5cm / 2in wide soft-bristle pastry brush for egg washing croissants and buns.

Silicone spatula
Heat-proof silicone spatula for creams and caramels.

Spray bottle
For spraying syrups with a fine mist to achieve a glossy finish and to apply an even coating of infused syrups.

Fine metal mesh sieves
For carefully sifting sugars and flours for pastry batters.

Extra fine shaker sieve
Shaker with extra fine metal mesh sieve for dusting icing sugar or cocoa powder.

Piping bags
Plastic or reusable canvas piping bags can be used for most pastry recipes.

Piping nozzles
Various nozzles in many shapes, sizes and styles provide a rich palette to give your own signature to cakes and tarts. Smooth round 13mm / 0.5in tips and 10mm / 0.4in star tips are most frequently used in the bakery.

Acetate
For supporting cakes, food safe acetate is very helpful.

Bread baskets, oblong or round for 800–900g dough

Supporting shaped loaves of higher hydrations, linen lined cane baskets or wood pulp unlined baskets are best. Alternatively, metal bowls or wicker baskets of a similar size can be used. For our shaped loaves you can adjust the final dough weight to suit your preferred basket size.

Pizza stone
A thick high-quality pizza stone will greatly improve the results of baking sourdough buns or flat breads in the home oven. The stone will help to hold and transfer the heat evenly to the bottom of the dough and provide a more even bake and a better crust.

Cast iron Dutch oven
For bread baking at home, a cast iron Dutch oven provides a simple solution for baking individual loaves with a beautiful crust, good volume and no need for additional steam pans in the oven.

Pizza peel
Gently transferring sourdough buns or flat bread to the oven is an exciting moment. A metal or wooden pizza peel will greatly ease the process of transferring the carefully-cared-for dough onto the baking stone in the oven. We suggest a peel roughly the same size as your pizza stone.

Scoring knives
To give the final touch and your personal signature to the shaped loaves, a scoring blade or lame with a high-quality double-edged razor is suggested.

Peeler and microplane
A sharp peeler and a microplane are frequently used to bring out the best of the citrus season.

Assortment of ring cutters
Great for punching out discs of sablé pastry, developing your own cookie sizes or experimenting with different styles of lamination.

Tart rings, cake moulds, baking tins
The ratios, textures and taste of our pastries have a direct relationship with the size and material of the baking moulds we use. For most of our products we have carefully experimented with and developed the balance that we find works for us. The moulds listed below and those stated in the recipes are the exact sizes we use. If you have other shapes and sizes, the process of adjusting the cakes and tarts can promise to be a rewarding experience.

Stainless steel rings
5cm / 2in high, 6cm / 2.4in diameter

Bottomless perforated tart rings
2cm / 0.8in high, 7cm / 2.8in diameter

Carbon steel tart tins with tapered edges
2cm / 0.8in high, 8.5cm / 3.3in diameter

Coated aluminium fluted brioche tins
4cm / 1.5in high, 11cm / 4.4in diameter

Copper tarte tatin pan
5cm / 2in × 24cm / 9.4in

Aluminium fluted tart mould
35cm long × 11cm wide, 2.5cm deep / 14 × 4.4 × 1in

Aluminium cake tin
6cm / 2.4in × 25.5cm / 10in

Stainless steel cake tin
43cm × 36cm × 1cm / 17 × 14.2 × 0.4in

SPECIALTY

Silicone Silpat baking mat with raised edges
43 × 36 × 1cm / 17 × 14.2 × 0.4in. Perfect for cake sponges that require precise specifications.

Canele tins
In copper, 4.5cm / 1.8in high, 4.5cm / 1.8in diameter.

Fluted pasta wheel
A fluted wheel can be used for cutting decorative patterns out of marzipan or sablé pastries.

Japanese spiralizer mandolin
We employ a spiralizer for the most delicate slicing of apples.

Blowtorch
A good quality adjustable blowtorch is a great tool to have on hand for tarts or caramelising slices of banana.

BREAD

DANISH RYE BREAD
MORNING BREAD
COUNTRY LOAF
SESAME LOAF
SOURDOUGH ROLLS
MILK BUNS
BAGUETTES
KAMUT CRISP BREAD

A thick slice of freshly baked sourdough bread, still warm with a generous amount of cold butter melting on top, is one of the simplest yet most comforting bites that exist and is something most of us have encountered. Bread is made from a wide variety of grains, in different shapes and sizes across the world. Many of them have a strong identity often connected to their heritage which is what we strive to express at the bakery. In Denmark we have rye bread. A cornerstone for the entire country, in its bricklike shape, made from rye flour and several seeds and grains, this is one of our essential breads and is an inevitable part of Danish culture. For the sourdough loaves we work with a variety of heirloom grain varieties, a good amount of wholegrain, which both adds flavour and depth. Qualities, that to us define the style of bread we love. The country loaf and sourdough rolls are a great example of this. They are the perfect partner to any meal but very much a meal of their own. Hearty and flavourful. Every Friday baguettes come fresh out the oven after lunch. Crispy on the outside, soft and airy on the inside. A real treat that marks the beginning of the weekend.

Flour selection

We are fortunate to work with farmers and millers who share our commitment to craft, from the rich soils of Denmark and southern Sweden. Our bread recipes are anchored in ancient grains – einkorn, spelt, rye and Öland – each contributing its unique character. These flours are what shape the identity of our bread.

The rye, einkorn, spelt and Öland are milled slowly on a Zentrofan vortex mill, producing a fine, whole-grain flour that brings a unique quality to each loaf. The beauty of these grains is that they allow us to work with a high percentage of whole grains, while still achieving a bread that is light, moist and tender. Using such flours requires a delicate balance, as hydration and mixing times must be adjusted to meet their demands. The key to consistency is repetition and constant attention to changes in the dough, combined with a stable, high-quality base flour, which helps to mitigate the natural variability of whole-grain flours.

For our cakes, buns and pastries, we opt for organic white roller-milled flour with 11% protein. For laminated products, a stronger flour with 12% protein ensures the right texture and structure.

Selecting your flour for our recipes will naturally require some experimentation to find similar flours to those we use in Denmark. Below is a rough guide for approximations of roller-milled white flours that you can typically use.

Flour for buns, breads and cakes is an organic 11% protein roller-milled white flour. Roughly equivalent to:

› French Type 55
› German Type 550
› Italian Type 0
› North American All-Purpose Flour
› United Kingdom Plain Flour

Flour for lamination

We use a relatively high-protein Danish roller-milled white flour, 12% protein. This flour provides a bit more stability for our laminated dough.

› French Type 55
› German Type 812
› Italian Type 1
› North American Bread Flour
› United Kingdom Bread Flour

Adopting a sourdough or starting from scratch

We recommend adopting a healthy well-cared for sourdough from your local bakery, as it is likely to produce a more stable fermentation. After adopting a sourdough, it will still take some time for it to adjust to your environment and baking routine.

If desired, it's possible to start a new sourdough culture from scratch that can adapt to your home environment, flour and baking habits. Start with a clean glass 500ml jar with a loose-fitting lid. Mix 20g of whole-grain rye flour with 20g water. Check the flour temperature and adjust the water temperature so that after mixing the blend is between 28–30°C / 82–86°F.

Store the jar in a warm place ideally about 28–30°C / 82–86°F and leave for 24 hours. Discard 30g of the mixture, and add another 20g of water and 20g of rye flour to the jar. Repeat this process of feeding and discarding for 5–6 days until the sourdough begins to smell acidic and rises consistently. After the culture becomes stable, follow the maintenance recommendations below.

Sourdough maintenance

Our sourdough is the very foundation of our bread. It is refreshed three times a day, always kept at 28–30°C / 82–86°F and primarily fed with white and rye flours. It lives, breathes and is cared for by the whole team. Our schedule follows a rhythm that aligns with the flow of our daily work, but feel free to adjust as needed to suit your baking. The key principle is finding a consistent routine that works best for your baking schedule, avoiding refrigeration and aiming for a fermentation temperature of about 28 to 30°C / 82–86°F. (see advice on proving page 32)

Each feeding is designed to ensure a fully active sourdough. To calculate the water temperature for each feeding, take the target temperature of 28°C / 82°F, multiply by 3, then subtract the actual room and flour temperatures. This will give you the approximate water temperature needed to bring the mixture to the desired temperature. If the required water temperature is above 35°C / 95°F, it is recommended to first blend the flour and water together before adding the sourdough.

For the starter build stated in the bread recipes, the required ripe sourdough should generally be built overnight and then fed again as stated in the recipes 3–4 hours before the beginning of mixing.

For example, if you plan to mix the following morning, feed your sourdough 9–12 hours before with:

› 90g of white flour
› 10g rye flour
› 5g ripe sourdough
› 100g water

The following morning the sourdough should be ripe and can be used to build the starter as required in the bread recipes.

For us, a well-fed, vibrant sourdough is the heart of good bread. It's important that it is always fully active before mixing. If baking less frequently, you might need to feed the starter at least three times before use.

BREAD PROCESS

Mixing
Our recipes are designed for mixing with spiral and stand mixers. Using a stand mixer with a dough hook or paddle attachment will achieve the best results. Most of the doughs can also be mixed by hand, however it will be more challenging to achieve a consistent result.

Proving
Temperature and humidity control is key to achieving a great result, for both sourdough and yeast-leavened products. For maintaining sourdough starters, bulk fermentation of bread dough, and final proving of yeasted products, it is important to maintain a temperature of 28–30°C / 82–86°F.

In the home kitchen, this can be achieved by using a switched-off oven as a proving area. Put a bowl of hot water, 70–80°C / 158–176°F, in the lower section of the oven, then place the product that requires warmth on the middle rack. Check the air temperature and change the water every 30–40 minutes to maintain the temperature. To prevent dry skins from forming on pastry products, lightly mist the surface with a water spray bottle.

Alternatively, using a large pot with warm water (40–50°C / 104–122°F), place the tray of products on top of the pot and gently cover with plastic or tea towels.

Breadmaking
All of our products are typically baked in a stone-deck oven using high temperatures and steam injection. However, if you don't have access to that, there are other options:

Pizza stone and steam tins
Preheat a baking stone on the oven's middle rack for 45 minutes to 1 hour at the baking temperature prescribed in the recipe.

Prepare two metal loaf tins. Boil a kettle with water. A few minutes before loading the oven, boil the water and pour it into each loaf tin till half full. Place the tins in the oven on the bottom.

If baking rye bread or sourdough buns, this method will achieve a good result.

Dutch-oven pot method
Preheat a large, heavy-bottomed Dutch oven or enameled cast-iron pot with the lid on in the oven for 1 hour before baking.

When the pot is preheated, take it out of the oven, removing the lid. Prepare a small round of baking paper in the same size as the lid. Place the baking paper on the preheated lid and gently transfer the proved loaf from the bread basket to the baking paper. Cover the lid with the pot and carefully return it to the middle rack of the oven. Follow the temperatures provided in the recipe.

This method is ideal for baking a single loaf of bread as the steam is trapped in the pot and a good crust is formed, without the need for steam pans.

Dough mixing
The art of mixing is one of constant adaptation and repetition. Each day, we adjust the hydration, mixing times and shaping techniques, responding to the unique properties of each batch of flour, as well as the required temperature and humidity. A steady and consistent sourdough feeding routine is essential, along with carefully managing dough and fermentation temperatures.

For most recipes – except for rye bread – the target dough temperature after mixing should be between 28–30°C / 82–86°F. To estimate the correct water temperature, multiply 28 by 4, then subtract the flour temperature, room temperature and sourdough temperature. Finally, subtract 8 for the heat generated by friction during mixing.

For example: with a flour temperature of 20°C / 68°F, room temperature of 25°C / 77°F, and sourdough at 28°C / 82°F, your water temperature should be about 31°C / 88°F.

$28 \times 4 = 112 - (20+25+28+8) = 31$

Autolyse
For all of the bread recipes, except for the rye bread, the flour and water is first mixed till combined and rested for at least 30 minutes. This stage helps to reduce the final mixing time, allows the flour to hydrate and activates the enzymes which begin breaking down the protein and starch.

Mixing

After adding the sourdough to the dough, the hydration should be checked and adjusted depending on the flour. After adding the salt, slowly pour a thin stream of water into the dough while mixing if extra water is needed.

Preshaping

For our highly hydrated doughs we use water instead of flour to divide the dough and preshape it round. This technique takes some practice, but to work with such wet doughs without extra flour can be very satisfying. For preshaping, turn the dough out onto a work surface with a thin layer of water spread on the surface. Wet your fingertips and, using a pastry card or metal dough scraper, divide and scale the dough to the desired weight. Then gently round the dough using the tension of the dough on the table and rotating and tucking the dough under itself, creating tension in the surface. Allow the dough to rest before the final shaping. Alternatively, the shaped loaf can be transferred directly to a well-oiled baking tin.

Final shaping and alternatives

Practice and repetition are the keys to shaping. While adapting to a new flour mix, if the dough for the dinner bread becomes too slack, it can also be proved and baked in a bread tin. We constantly vary our shaping techniques, responding to the tension of the dough and the extensibility, elasticity and texture of every mix.

Shaping

Lightly flour your work surface and the top surface of your loaf. Using a large dough scraper, release the dough from the work surface and flip it over, so that the top skin is down onto the table. Then take hold of the left and right top corners and slide the dough on the work surface, folding the top half down to the bottom. Immediately after, take hold of the bottom corners and stretch and fold the bottom third back up onto the middle of the dough. Quickly slide your hands under the folded dough and pick it up from the bottom, lift and gently squeeze the left and right side together before transferring the dough to a well-floured, bread basket. This will create tension and structure.

DANISH RYE BREAD

Makes one loaf

Rye grain sprouts
300g water
140g rye grain

Starter build (page 30)
70g white wheat flour, 11% protein
70g water
28g ripe sourdough starter

Dough
220g water
50g dark ale beer
60g buttermilk
110g sourdough (from above)
7g salt
4.5g Husk
175g rye grain sprouts
125g white flour
48g rye flour
5g dark malt powder
18g sunflower seeds
18g pumpkin seeds
40g sesame seeds
48g linseed
24g rye flakes
Melted salted butter for the tin

Starter build

Ingredients	*Weight*	*Baker's %*
White wheat flour	70g	100%
Water	70g	100%
Ripe sourdough	28g	40%

Final dough

Ingredients	*Weight*	*Baker's %*
White flour	125g	72%
Rye flour	50g	28%
Water	220g	128%
Buttermilk	60g	35%
Dark ale beer	50g	29%
Sourdough (from build)	110g	64%
Rye grain sprouts	175g	100%
Salt	7g	4.0%
Husk	5g	2.6%
Dark malt powder	5g	2.9%
Sunflower seeds	20g	10%
Pumpkin seeds	20g	10%
Sesame seeds	40g	23%
Linseed	50g	28%

Our rye bread is a cherished part of the bakery; it's constantly evolving as we seek incremental improvements. The process that we have developed is a result of the desired taste, texture, nutritional content, and keeping quality, combined with how it suits our workflow and daily rhythm in the bakery. There are many aspects of the recipe which deviate from traditional approaches to rye bread baking. We invite you to take this formula as a starting point and adapt it to your own preferences.

Preparation
Two days before mixing the dough, prepare the rye sprouts. Larger batches of rye sprouts can be made and stored in the freezer.

Soak 140g rye grain in 300g of warm water. Drain after 12 hours and leave to sprout in a warm space for 24–30 hours until the grains are tender, sweet, and the first tips of the sprouts have emerged.

→

Day 1

Starter build
3–4 hours before starting the final mix, mix the starter flour, water and sourdough together and allow it to ferment between 28 and 30°C / 82 and 86°F.

Final mix
When the starter is ripe and easily floats in warm water, begin the mix.

In a Kitchen Aid mixer or similar, mix for 5 minutes at slow speed water, beer, buttermilk, sourdough from above (check that it floats in warm water and is fully ripe), salt and Husk together. Let the mixture rest for 10 minutes.

Add the rye sprouts, flour, dark malt powder and all of the seeds into the mixing bowl. Mix at slow speed for 5 minutes. Scrape down the sides and check for any unincorporated flour. Finish the mixing at second speed for 10–12 minutes until the mix forms a thick batter. Transfer the rye mixture to an airtight, well-oiled container.

Leave it for 1 hour at room temperature, then store in the fridge for 18–24 hours.

Day 2
Coat your rye bread loaf tin with melted butter and gently transfer the dough directly from the fridge to the tin.

Cover the tin well and allow the dough to rise in a warm, humid place for about 5–7 hours, depending on the temperature (see advice on proving page 32). Place a bowl of warm water in your oven, to help maintain the temperature.

The dough will be ready when the loaf rises about 30% and has air bubbles on the surface. Remove the loaf from the oven, if used for the rising process.

Preheat the oven to 210°C / 410°F on top and bottom heat setting. Brush the top of the loaf with water.

Bake the loaf for 55–65 minutes. Check the centre of the loaf with a temperature probe. It should be at least 97°C / 207°F. If not, add additional baking time.

Remove the tin from the oven, take the loaf out of the tin and place the loaf on a cooling rack. We recommend waiting at least a few hours before attempting to slice the loaf.

If stored in a bread box, the rye bread will typically last 4–5 days.

MORNING BREAD

Makes one loaf

Starter build (page 30)
50g white flour, 11% protein
20g whole-grain rye flour
70g water
28g ripe sourdough

Dough
210g white flour, 11% protein
70g whole-grain einkorn flour
70g white Öland flour
45g whole-grain rye flour
12g salt
350g water
140g sourdough

Dusting
20g whole-grain rye flour

Starter build

Ingredients	*Weight* (adjusted)	*Baker's %*
White flour	50g	70%
Whole-grain rye flour	20g	30%
Water	70g	100%
Ripe sourdough	28g	40%

Final dough

Ingredients	*Weight* (adjusted)	*Baker's %*
White flour	210g	53.0%
Whole-grain einkorn	70g	18.0%
White Öland flour	70g	18.0%
Whole-grain rye flour	45g	11.0%
Water	350g	89%
Salt	12g	3.0%
Sourdough (from build)	140g	35%

Starter build
3–4 hours before starting the final mix, mix the starter flour, water and sourdough together and allow it to ferment between 24–26°C / 75–79°F (see page 32 for advice on proving).

Final dough
Scale the flours together in a bowl. Scale the salt and water separately. Pour the water into the mixing bowl of a stand mixer and add all of the flour. Mix for 5 minutes at slow speed. Scrape the sides of the bowl down and make sure there is no dry flour. Mix again for 1 minute slowly. Rest the dough for 35 minutes.

Add the ripe sourdough (it should be fully ripe and easily float in warm water). Mix for 10 minutes at slow speed to combine the sourdough and gently develop the dough. Add the salt. Mix for another 10 minutes at slow speed. The dough should become smooth and elastic and come away from the sides of the bowl. Transfer the dough to a well-oiled container. Check the final dough temperature (target 28–30°C / 82–86°F). Store the dough in a warm place to prove.

Stretch and fold the dough 2 times in the first 40 minutes (see guide in the introduction to the bread section). After the second fold, leave the dough to rise for 2–2.5 hours in a warm place.

→

Shaping
Prepare a well-oiled loaf tin.

Gently wet your work surface. Turn the dough out onto the table and gently round the dough to create tension in the surface. In one motion, pick up the rounded dough from the table and transfer it into the loaf tin. Cover the tin and leave the dough in a warm place to rise for 3–4 hours.

When it has risen 30–40%, transfer the loaf to the fridge (gently covered). Leave it in the fridge for 10–18 hours before baking.

Baking
Preheat your oven to 250°C / 482°F using the top and bottom heat setting.

When the oven is ready, remove the loaf from the fridge. Dust the top of the loaf with whole-grain rye flour. Using a sharp serrated paring knife, make a straight cut from end to end of the loaf, approximately 1.5cm / 0.6in deep.

Place the loaf in the oven and bake with steam pans for 30 minutes (see page 32 for steam techniques). Turn the loaf and continue baking for another 15 minutes. Check the colour of the top and the internal temperature. When it reaches 97°C / 207°F, the loaf is finished baking.

Remove the tin from the oven, take the loaf out of the tin and place the loaf it on a cooling rack and wait at least 1 hour before slicing the bread.

COUNTRY LOAF

Makes one large loaf

Starter build (page 30)
70g white flour, 11% protein
10g rye flour
70g water
10g ripe sourdough

Dough
175g white flour, 11% protein
120g whole-grain Dala wheat flour
100g strong white flour, 12% protein
85g whole-grain spelt flour
340g water 1 (first addition)
145g sourdough (from above)
14g salt
20g water 2 (final mixing)

For dusting
50g semolina flour
50g white flour

Starter build

Ingredients	*Weight*	*Baker's %*
White flour	70g	90%
Rye flour	10g	11%
Water	70g	100%
Ripe sourdough	10g	10%

Final dough

Ingredients	*Weight*	*Baker's %*
White flour	175g	31.3%
Whole-grain Dala wheat flour	120g	21.4%
Strong white flour 12% protein	100g	17.9%
Whole-grain spelt flour	85g	15.2%
Water 1 (first addition)	340g	60.7%
Water 2 (final mixing)	20g	3.6%
Sourdough (from above)	145g	25.9%
Salt	14g	2.5%

Starter build
3–4 hours before mixing.
Mix the flour, water and ripe sourdough together in a bowl.
Target temperature 28–30°C / 82–86°F.

Mixing
Scale the flours together in a bowl. Scale the salt and water separately. Target temperature for the final dough is 30°C / 86°F.

Pour the water into the mixing bowl and add all of the flour. Mix for 5 minutes at a slow speed using the dough hook attachment. Scrape sides of the bowl and make sure there is no dry flour. Mix again for 1 minute slowly. Add the ripe sourdough (it should be fully ripe and easily float in warm water), add the salt and extra water and mix for 10 minutes at a slow speed. Scrape down the sides of the bowl. Continue mixing for 2 minutes at a fast speed until the dough comes together and just begins to clear the sides of the bowl. Transfer the dough to a well-oiled container.

Store in a warm place ideally 28°C / 82°F. Fold the dough three times at 20-minute intervals. After the last fold, allow to rise another 1.5 hours. Then transfer to the refrigerator (4–5°C / 39–41°F) to limit the fermentation and rest till the following day.

→

Shaping
Remove the country dough from the fridge and check the fermentation, it should have almost doubled in volume from the point of mixing. If it seems under-fermented, leave it out for 30 minutes to rise.

Prepare a tea towel and a thin cutting board that is about 20cm / 8in wide. Place the tea towel onto the board, dust the tea towel with flour. This will be used to support the country bread while it rises.

Generously dust your work surface with white flour. Dust the top of the country dough in the container and use a plastic dough scraper to release the edges. Flip over the container and allow the dough to fall out onto the work surface. It is important to avoid it folding onto itself.

Dust the top of the dough with flour. And using your hands, slide and shuffle the dough in the flour, left to right, and up and down on the worksurface. The goal is to gently catch the flour in the bottom surface of the dough, forming striations.

Using your hand and a dough scraper, pick up the dough from the table without flipping it over (maintaining the same orientation) and place it onto the floured tea towel. Depending on the fermentation, rest the dough on the tea towel for about 20 minutes at room temperature, then in the fridge for 30 minutes.

→

Baking

1 hour before baking, preheat the oven with a baking stone to 300°C / 572°F (or highest possible temperature) on top and bottom heat setting, or if using a Dutch oven, preheat the Dutch oven.

5 minutes before baking, place steam pans into the oven (see steam guide, page 32). Lightly dust the surface of the loaf with semolina flour. Dust the pizza peel with semolina flour. Gently flip over the loaf from the tea towel and place the loaf on the pizza peel. Transfer the loaf into the oven and pour boiling water into the steam pan.

Lower the heat to 230°C / 446°F and bake for 15 minutes. After 15 minutes remove the steam pans from the oven. If using a Dutch oven, remove the lid after about 20 minutes. Continue baking for 20 minutes without the lid if using a Dutch oven. Turn the loaf and continue baking till the crust is crisp and darkly caramelised. Remove from the oven using the pizza peel or remove the loaf from the Dutch oven and place on a wire rack to cool.

SESAME LOAF

Makes one loaf

Starter build (page 30)
70g white flour, 11% protein
70g water
28g ripe sourdough

Dough
250g white Kornby flour (equivalent to T80)
45g white Öland flour
70g whole-grain spelt flour
20g whole-grain rye flour
280g water
12g salt
140g sourdough

20g white sesame seeds (roasted, for folding into the dough)
100g white sesame seeds (for coating)

Dusting
100g white flour
50g semolina flour

Starter build

Ingredients	*Weight*	*Baker's %*
White flour	70g	100%
Water	70g	100%
Ripe sourdough	28g	40%

Final dough

Ingredients	*Weight*	*Baker's %*
White flour	250g	65%
White Öland flour	45g	12%
Whole-grain spelt flour	70g	18%
Whole-grain rye flour	20g	5%
Water	280g	73%
Salt	12g	3%
Ripe sourdough (from build)	140g	37%

Recipe variations
20g roasted mixed seeds (7g sunflower seeds, 7g pumpkin seeds, 3g golden linseed, 3g brown linseed).

50g roasted walnuts. For the best flavour, prepare the nuts the day before. Soak them in warm water for 2 hours, changing the water every 30 minutes. After soaking, drain and dry the walnuts. Then roast them in the oven at 180°C / 356°F until evenly brown. Let the walnuts cool to room temperature and break them by hand into smaller pieces.

Topping variations
50g mixed seeds (18g sunflower seeds, 18g pumpkin seeds, 7g golden linseed, 7g brown linseed).

50g rye flakes for walnut bread.

→

Starter build
3–4 hours before mixing, mix flour, water and ripe sourdough together in a bowl. Target temperature 28–30°C / 82–86°F.

Seeds
Preheat the oven to 180°C / 356°F on top and bottom heat setting. Roast the sesame seeds for about 10 minutes until evenly golden brown. Allow them to cool, then add 10g water and mix into the sesame.

Dough
Scale the flours together in a bowl. Scale salt and water separately. Pour the water into the mixing bowl of a stand mixer and add all of the flour. Mix for 5 minutes at slow speed. Scrape the sides of the bowl down and make sure there is no dry flour. Mix again for 1 minute slowly. Rest the dough for 35 minutes.

Add the ripe sourdough (it should be fully ripe and easily float in warm water). Mix for 10 minutes at slow speed to combine the sourdough and gently develop the dough. Add the salt. Mix for another 10 minutes at slow speed. Check the dough and mix for 1–2 minutes at second speed. The dough should be smooth and elastic and come away from the sides of the bowl. Transfer the dough to a well-oiled container. Check the final dough temperature (target 28–30°C / 82–86°F). Set the dough aside in a warm place to prove.

Variations
If you plan to make the mixed seed variation, mix the seeds with 10g of water and allow to absorb for 2 minutes. For the walnut variation, mix the nuts with 25g of water. Then when stretching and folding the dough, sprinkle the additions into the dough until evenly incorporated.

→

Fold the dough three times in the first 40 minutes (see guide in the introduction to the bread section, page 33). After the third fold, leave the dough to rise for 2–2.5 hours in a warm space.

Gently wet your work surface and turn the dough out of the container. Preshape the dough into a round ball using a pastry card, until it has an even tension. Transfer the dough to a baking tray and leave it to rest for 20–30 minutes in a warm place.

On a 9 × 9cm / 3.5 × 3.5in plate or container lid, spread the unroasted white sesame seeds.

Prepare a bread basket; however, you do not need to dust it with flour. Flour the work surface and, using the pastry card, carefully transfer the rested dough to the table. Shape the dough following the guide (page 33). After shaping, place the shaped loaf on the work surface. Lightly pat the surface with water. Using a pastry card, pick up the loaf and roll the surface in the white sesame seeds. Transfer the loaf directly to the bread basket with the seam-side up.

Variations
If making the mixed seed or walnut loaf, spread the seeds or rye flakes on the plate.

Allow the loaf to rise for 2–3 hours in a warm place. When increased by 20–30% in volume, lightly cover with a tea towel and transfer to the fridge.

Baking and scoring
45 minutes to 1 hour before baking, preheat the oven with a baking stone to 300°C / 572°F (or highest possible temperature) on top and bottom heat setting.

5 minutes before baking, place steam pans in the oven (see steam guide, page 32).

Lightly dust the surface of the loaf and the pizza peel with semolina flour. Gently flip over the bread basket and place the loaf on the pizza peel. Score the top of the bread using a razor blade. Transfer the loaf to the oven and pour boiling water into the steam pan.

Lower the heat to 230°C / 446°F and bake for 15 minutes. After 15 minutes, remove the steam pans from the oven. Continue baking for 20 minutes. Turn the loaf to ensure even baking and continue baking till the crust is crisp and golden brown.

Remove the loaf from the oven using the peel and place it on a wire rack to cool. Leave it to cool for 1 hour before slicing.

SOURDOUGH ROLLS

Makes 10 rolls

Starter build (page 30)
85g water
85g white flour, 11% protein
32g ripe sourdough

Dough
240g white flour, 11% protein
85g einkorn whole-grain flour
85g white Öland flour
70g whole-grain rye flour
14g salt
380g water
170g sourdough

100g white flour, for dusting

Starter build

Ingredients	*Weight*	*Baker's %*
White wheat flour	85g	100%
Water	85g	100%
Ripe sourdough	32g	40%

Final Dough

Ingredients	*Weight*	*Baker's %*
White flour	240g	50.0%
Whole-grain einkorn flour	85g	18%
White Öland flour	85g	18%
Whole-grain rye flour	70g	14%
Water	380g	80%
Salt	14g	3%
Sourdough (from build)	170g	35%

Variation, additions to fold into dough:
50g roasted white sesame seeds.

50g roasted mixed seeds, for example sunflower seeds, pumpkin seeds, golden linseed, brown linseed.

Seeds for topping
50g white sesame seeds.

50g mixed seeds, unroasted, for example sunflower seeds, pumpkin seeds, golden linseed, brown linseed.

Starter build
3–4 hours before mixing the dough, mix flour, water, and ripe sourdough together in a bowl. Target temperature 28–30°C / 82–86°F.

Dough
Scale the flours together in a bowl. Scale the salt and water separately. Pour the water into the mixing bowl of a stand mixer and add all of the flour. Mix for 5 minutes at slow speed. Scrape the sides of the bowl down and make sure there is no dry flour. Mix again for 1 minute slowly. Rest the dough for 35 minutes.

Add the ripe sourdough (it should be fully ripe and easily float in warm water). Mix for 10 minutes at slow speed to combine the sourdough and gently develop the dough. Add the salt. Mix for another 10 minutes at slow speed. The dough should become smooth and elastic and come away from the sides of the bowl. Transfer the dough to a well-oiled container. Check the final dough temperature (target 28–30°C / 82–86°F). Set the dough aside in a warm place to prove.

→

Variations
If you plan to make the roasted sesame or roasted seed rolls, mix the 50g of seeds with 25g of water and allow to absorb for 2 minutes. Then, when stretching and folding the dough, sprinkle the seeds into the dough.

Fold the dough 2 times in the first 40 minutes (see guide in the introduction to the bread section, page 33). After the second fold, leave the dough to rise for 2–2.5 hours in a warm space. Move the dough to the fridge and store it for 10–18 hours.

Dividing and baking
Preheat your oven with a baking stone to 300°C / 572°F (highest temperature possible, 280°C / 536°F can also be used with adjustments to baking time). Prepare a baking paper to the size of your pizza stone and lightly flour it.

Remove the dough from the fridge. Using a flour sieve, dust a work surface generously with white flour. Remove the lid of the container and flour the top surface of the dough. Using a plastic pastry scraper, gently release the sides of the dough from the container. Flip the container over and allow the dough to fall evenly onto the work surface. It is important to avoid folding the dough onto itself. Dust the top of the dough with flour.

Variations
If making sesame or mixed seed rolls, no flour will be required. Spread 50g of seeds directly onto the unfloured dough and thickly coat the top surface with the seeds.

Using a pastry card, cut the dough into even squares, approximately 110g each. Carefully transfer the sourdough rolls to the floured baking paper, leaving about 3–4cm / 1.2–1.5in between them, depending on the size of your baking stone. Leave the rolls to rest 10–15 minutes on the baking paper before loading them into the oven.

Bake the rolls in two batches. 2 minutes before loading, place steam pans into the bottom of the oven (see steam guide, page 32). Load the rolls into the oven using a pizza peel to transfer the rolls from the baking paper to the baking stone. Bake for 8 minutes at 280–300°C / 536–572°F (depending on maximum oven temperature). Turn each roll to ensure even baking and bake for 4–5 minutes until the crust is set and golden brown.

Remove the rolls from the oven onto a cooling rack. Allow the oven to reheat fully before loading the next batch of rolls.

MILK BUNS

Makes 10 buns

Dough
15g scald (page 318)
135g baking potatoes, peeled and boiled
410g white flour, 12% protein
35g white sugar
10g salt
110g cold water
45g milk, 3.5% fat
15g fresh yeast
50g salted butter, cold
10g salted butter, for brushing

Dough

Ingredients	*Weight*	*Baker's %*
Scald	15g	3.7%
Baking potatoes (after peeling & boiling)	135g	33%
White flour	410g	100%
White sugar	35g	8.5%
Salt	10g	2.5%
Cold water	110g	27%
Milk, 3.5% fat	45g	11%
Fresh yeast	15g	3.7%
Butter (salted)	50g	12%

Preparations
A few hours before mixing the dough, prepare the scald and potatoes. Make sure they have fridge temperature before mixing.

Potatoes
Peel and boil the potatoes for about 25 minutes until soft. Drain and cool in the fridge.

Dough
Scale all the dry ingredients together into a bowl and set aside. Scale the potatoes, scald, milk, fresh yeast and butter cut into cubes into the bowl of a stand mixer. Mix at fast speed with the hook attachment for 5 minutes until the potatoes are mostly broken down into a smooth consistency. Add the water and dry ingredients. Mix at slow speed for 10 minutes. Scrape the sides of the bowl down and clear the hook. Resume mixing for 5 minutes at slow speed. Mix for 5–6 minutes at second speed until the dough pulls away from the sides of the bowl and is supple and elastic.

Remove the dough from the mixer, form 1 large ball and transfer it to an oiled airtight container to rest overnight in the fridge at 4–5°C / 39–41°F.

12–24 hours later
Remove the dough from the fridge. Divide it into 80g balls (or your preferred size), carefully roll round and place them close together, about 1.5cm / 0.6in apart, on a baking tray lined with baking paper. Alternatively leave about 3–4cm / 1.2–1.5in of space for individual buns.

Proving
Place the buns into a warm, humid space (see proving advice page 32). It will take between 1 and 1.5 hours for the buns to rise (depending on the exact temperature).

→

Baking

Preheat the oven for 30 minutes to 215°C / 420°F with the top, bottom and fan elements.

5 minutes before loading the buns into the oven, place two steam pans in the oven (see steam guide, page 32). Put the tray with the buns in the oven and bake for 8 minutes. Check and rotate the tray for even baking, then continue baking for about 4–5 minutes until the buns are golden brown.

Butter glaze

Melt the butter and evenly brush the buns with the melted butter.

BAGUETTES

Makes 6–7 demi-baguettes

Dough
650g water
660g white flour, 11% protein
190g white Kornby flour
150g whole-grain spelt flour
19g salt
6g fresh yeast
125g water (for final mixing)

For dusting
50g semolina flour
50g white flour

Variation with sesame
50g white sesame, for roasting
200g white sesame, for coating

Dough

Ingredients	*Weight*	*Baker's %*
White flour	660g	66%
White Kornby flour	190g	19%
Whole-grain spelt flour	150g	15%
Total flour	1000g	100%
Water 1 (first addition)	650g	65%
Water 2 (final mix)	125g	12.5%
Total water	775g	77.5%
Salt	19g	1.9%
Fresh yeast	6g	0.6%

Day 1
If you plan to make sesame baguettes, start by roasting 50g of sesame seeds until golden brown, add 25g of water and allow to cool.

Mixing
Scale the flours together in a bowl. Calculate the water temperature for a final temperature of about 24–25°C / 75–77°F (page 32). Pour the water into the mixing bowl of a stand mixer and add all of the flour. Mix for 5 minutes at slow speed using the dough hook attachment. Scrape the sides of the bowl and make sure there is no dry flour left. Mix again for 1 minute slowly. Rest the dough for 35 minutes.

Add the fresh yeast and salt. Mix for 5 minutes at slow speed to combine the salt and yeast and gently develop the dough. Mix for another 10 minutes at slow to medium speed, adding the second water as slowly as possible during the final mixing. When the dough absorbs the water, continue adding in a thin stream. Once all the water is incorporated, increase the speed to medium-high for 2–3 more minutes. Mix until the dough becomes smooth and elastic and pulls away from the sides of the bowl.

Transfer the dough to a well-oiled container. Check the final dough temperature (target 24–25°C / 75–77°F). Place the dough in a warm place.

After 30 minutes, fold the dough, cover and place in the fridge at 4–5°C / 39–41°F. (If you are making sesame baguettes, gently fold in the roasted sesame seeds at this point.) Store overnight, 12–18 hours.

→

Day 2
Preheat the oven to 280°C / 536°F on top and bottom heat setting. Set up steam pans (page 32).

Dividing
Remove the baguette dough from the fridge, it should have doubled in volume overnight.

Using a flour sieve, dust your work surface generously with white flour. Remove the lid of the container and flour the top surface of the dough. With a plastic pastry scraper, gently release the sides of the dough from the container. Flip the container over and allow the dough to fall evenly onto the work surface. It is important to avoid folding the dough onto itself. Dust the top of the dough with flour. Using a scraper, cut the dough into even squares, approximately 6 pieces of 250g each.

Preshaping
Take the top of a square and fold the top section down to the centre in a straight line. Next, fold the bottom half up to the centre to meet the top section. Connect the seam in the centre applying gentle but firm pressure. Repeat with the remaining squares and allow them to rest a few minutes.

Final shaping
Prepare a tea towel and a thin cutting board that is about 20cm / 8in wide. Place the tea towel on the board and dust it with flour. This will help support the baguettes while they rise.

Lightly flour the work surface and prepare to shape the baguettes. Take the preshaped piece from the table and place it seam-side down on the dusted surface. Press gently across the length of the dough to degas slightly. Flip over the dough (seam-side now up) with the open edges on the left and right sides.

Take the top edge and fold it down to the centre of the dough, creating tension. This is the first step of forming the tube that will become the baguette. Rotate the dough 180° and fold the other edge down to the centre connecting the seam with firm pressure. Next, take the edge that you have just folded and fold it down again by a third onto the bottom section of the tube. Finally, take the top edge again and fold it down to the bottom edge of the dough, sealing the seam with the blade of your hand to connect the dough and form an even tube.

→

Lightly dust the tube with flour and, using even pressure, roll the dough out until the tube is about 20cm / 8in long. If desired, taper it by applying light pressure to the right and left ends and drawing out the points on both sides.

Roll the shaped baguette over, seam-side up, and transfer it to the floured tea towel. Fold the tea towel up to support the length of the baguette. Finish shaping the remaining baguettes.

If making the sesame baguettes:
Prepare a wide-low walled (about 15cm / 6in long) container with 200g of sesame seeds spread in an even layer. After shaping each baguette, wet a small area of the work surface and roll the top and sides of each baguette in water, then transfer it to the sesame seeds, coating the top and side.

Final proving
Allow the baguettes to rise for about 35–40 minutes at a room temperature of 25°C / 77°F. Transfer the baguettes to the fridge and chill for about 30 minutes.

Baking
Prepare a baking paper the same size as your pizza stone, place it on the pizza peel and lightly dust the paper with semolina flour. Use a small thin cutting board or similar rigid object to transfer the first three baguettes onto the baking paper. Using the tea towel, flip the baguette onto the board (seam up), then flip it over onto the baking paper (seam-side down), evenly spacing the baguettes. Use a razor blade to score each baguette end to end with a single cut.

Transfer the baguettes onto the stone. Steam the oven using steam pans (page 32). Bake for about 12 minutes at 280°C / 536°F on top and bottom heat setting. Check and turn each baguette and bake for 5 minutes more. Bake until the baguettes are golden brown with a darkly caramelised ear along the score.

KAMUT CRISP BREAD

Makes 6 pieces

Soaker
20g roasted kamut flakes
30g water

Starter build (page 30)
40g water
40g white flour, 11% protein
15g ripe sourdough

Final dough
65g white flour, 11% protein
65g whole-grain kamut flour
20g whole-grain rye flour
4g salt
55g water
65g ripe sourdough
1g fresh yeast
50g soaked kamut flakes (from above)

Starter build

Ingredients	*Weight*	*Baker's %*
White flour	40g	100%
Water	40g	100%
Ripe sourdough	15g	40%

Final dough

Ingredients	*Weight*	*Baker's %*
White flour	65g	42%
Whole-grain kamut flour	65g	42%
Whole-grain rye flour	25g	16%
Water	55g	35.5%
Salt	4g	2.5%
Fresh yeast	1g	0.6%
Sourdough (from build)	65g	42%
Roasted kamut flakes (soaker)	20g	13% (add-in)

Soaker
The day before mixing: roast the kamut flakes in the oven at 180°C / 356°F until golden brown and evenly toasted. Allow to cool and transfer the flakes to a sealable container. Mix with the water and leave to soak at room temperature overnight.

Starter build
3–4 hours before mixing the dough, mix flour, water and ripe sourdough together in a bowl. Target temperature 28–30°C / 82–86°F.

Dough
Scale all the dry ingredients together in a bowl, including the salt. Starting with the water, sourdough, yeast and soaked kamut flakes, mix all the ingredients together in the bowl of a stand mixer.

Mix for 5 minutes in slow speed until combined. Scrape the sides of the bowl down and check for any unincorporated flour. Mix for 2–3 minutes in second speed. The dough will come together, be firm and dense and not sticky to the touch. Transfer the dough to a container and store it in a warm place (28–30°C / 82–86°F) for 1 hour.

Divide the dough into 65g pieces and roll them into round balls. Place the balls on a lightly floured baking sheet, with 3–4cm between. Dust the top of the balls and, using another clean baking sheet or a cutting board, press the buns down, so that they flatten out into discs, about 2cm / 0.8in thick. Tightly cover the tray with plastic wrap or put in a large plastic bag. Place the tray in the fridge and store for 10–18 hours.

→

Day 2
Remove the dough from the fridge and allow it to come up to room temperature for 20–30 minutes.

Preheat the oven with a baking stone to the highest possible temperature. 300°C / 572°F is ideal.

Lightly flour your work surface. One at a time, begin rolling out the dough pieces. Roll the balls as thin as possible, flipping, dusting with flour and rotating them until a thin oblong shape is achieved, 1.5–2mm / 0.06–0.08in thick, and about 30cm / 12in long, 8cm / 3in wide. Dust the surface with flour and roll the docking tool over the surface. Alternatively, a fork can be used to prevent uneven rising.

Gently transfer each piece from the work surface to a floured pizza peel. Using the pizza peel, transfer the dough directly onto the preheated baking stone. Bake for 3 minutes at 300°C / 572°F. Carefully turn the crisp bread to allow even baking. Bake for another 2–3 minutes until the surface is golden brown.

Repeat with the remaining balls. If they become too warm while baking the first batch, return them to the fridge.

HE

LAMINATION

From the mixing of dough, to the forming of butter sheets, to laminating, dividing, rolling, placing on trays, proving, egg washing, egg washing again and finally baking, lamination is all about detail and care. From the soft, buttery centre to the brittle edges breaking down into flakes of thin, papery dough, the croissant is a pastry of its own category. We like them well-baked with a deeply caramelised crust. Our croissants, and all the variations we have at the bakery, feature almost every day, all year round. Together with a few other baked goods, they are a kind of testimony to consistency. The key is to respect the full process, temperatures, resting times and measurements, to ensure that they are of equal quality every day. Use the photos in correlation with the text, and the more you laminate, the more you'll see how fascinating this whole process can be.

CROISSANT DOUGH

Makes 10 croissants

180g milk, 3.5% fat
180g water
26g fresh yeast
670g white flour, 12% protein
80g white sugar
14g salt

Butter sheet
400g salted butter

Mixing
Scale and chill all of the ingredients a few hours before mixing. In the bakery we store the flour in the freezer. Put the milk, water and yeast into the bowl of a stand mixer. Add the flour, sugar and salt. Using the dough hook attachment, mix for 5 minutes at slow speed and scrape the sides of the bowl. Mix for another 3.5–4 minutes at second speed. The dough should come together but still be rough in texture.

Remove the dough from the mixer and shape it into a round ball. Using a bread knife, cut a cross about 1.5cm / 0.6in deep into the top of the dough. Press out the four corners to form a square. Using cling film or a large thick plastic bag, tightly wrap the dough. Transfer the dough directly to the fridge at the coldest setting possible, 1–2°C / 34–36°F. Store the dough for 12–18 hours before starting the lamination process.

Butter sheet
Remove the butter from the fridge and allow it to warm up for 45 minutes or so. It should be malleable but not spreadable soft. Cut the butter into strips and lay it out onto a baking paper in a rectangular shape. Place another baking paper on top and roll out the butter until forming a square about 16.5cm / 6.5in. Use the baking paper to fold the edges of the butter to create sharp angles. Make sure the butter sheet is as even as possible. Transfer the butter sheet to the fridge and chill briefly.

Locking in the butter (step 1, photos 3 and 4)
Classic croissant lamination consists of one single fold (otherwise known as a half turn) and one double fold (book turn). This will give a dough mass that has 12 layers of butter in total.

Remove the butter sheet from the fridge. The butter must be pliable, between 12–18°C / 54–64°F.

During this entire process, one of the most important things to consider is the temperature of the butter. It should always be at a 'working temperature'. This means that the butter is of similar consistency to the dough. If too cold, the butter will crack and break away from the dough mass, resulting in a loss of layer definition. If too warm, the butter will not be able to hold its shape and will result in uneven or sometimes non-existent layers.

For the following steps follow the photo guide on page 90–91: Remove the dough from the fridge and unwrap it. The working temperature for the dough should be between 1 and 3°C / 34–37°F. Lightly flour the work surface and roll out the dough with firm, even pressure until it is 1.5cm thick, 16.5cm wide and 34.5cm high / 0.6 × 6.5 × 13.6in.

→

During the entire lamination process, if you feel the dough is getting difficult to roll, shrinking back or getting too warm, you can always wrap it up again and return it to the fridge for 5–10 minutes. This is key to getting beautiful layers.

Take the butter sheet and place it on the bottom half of the rectangle. The butter should match the width of the dough. Fold the top half of the dough over the butter, forming a square. Using light, even pressure, press down on the mass to seal the butter to the dough.

Using a sharp paring knife, cut the seam where the dough was folded over so that all four sides of the dough are open and you can see the 3 layers: dough, butter, dough. At this stage, if the butter is beginning to melt or soften, wrap the dough tightly and place it in the fridge for 5 minutes.

Turn the dough 90 degrees clockwise and begin to roll the dough from left to right. If you feel the dough is sticking to the table, you can use a small amount of flour underneath. Roll the dough to 7mm thick, 16.5cm high and 68cm high / 0.3 × 6.5 × 26.8in (photo 5).

Single fold (photos 5–8)
Imagine the dough is made up of 3 sections. These sections are the left, middle and right of the rectangle. Fold the right section over the middle section, then fold the left section up over the right section. This is a single fold. You have now created your first 3 layers.

Rotate the dough 90 degrees. The 'open ends' of the dough will now be at the top and bottom of the piece. This is the orientation you will work with the dough for the next fold. Wrap the dough tightly in cling film and let it rest in the fridge for about 15–20 minutes.

Double fold (photos 9–16)
After this rest period, take the dough and place it on a very lightly floured surface. Make sure the dough is in the correct orientation as before. Using a sharp blade, cut open the folded seams on the left and right side. This will allow for a straighter layer formation.

Now begin rolling out the dough as before to 7mm thick, 16.5cm high and 72cm long / 0.3 × 6.5 × 28.3in, placing the dough in the fridge for a few minutes at any point if you feel it is getting too warm.

→

You will now perform the second and final fold of the dough, i.e double fold. For the double fold, imagine that the dough is now made up of 4 sections.

Take the dough from the right-side corners and fold it to the left to cover the middle three quarters of the dough. Now take the corners of the left quarter and fold it up to meet the edge of the folded side. Both ends should fully meet in the centre, leaving no gaps. (Photos 9–12).

Now cut along the folded seams on the left and right side of the dough. Gently roll the piece lengthwise from left to right until it is roughly 40cm / 15.7in long.

The final step of the double fold is to take the right half of the dough and fold it over to meet the left edge. (Photos 13-14). Finally, cut the folded seam to allow for a neater finish in the layers (photos 15-16).

Rotate the dough 90 degrees. This is the orientation the piece must be in when using for final pieces. You have now completed the lamination of the dough.

Resting
Wrap the dough tightly in cling film and rest it in the fridge for a minimum of 1 hour to give the gluten in the dough a chance to relax. This will make the dough easier to work with and prevent it from 'snapping back' when you try to roll it out for the last time.

This dough can now be rolled out to different dimensions and be used for the other laminated products in the book.

Lamination process
Our croissants are at the foundation of the daily routine in the bakery. We strive every day to achieve the best result we can. Every morning we find out if we have succeeded or need to adjust for the next batch. If we succeed, then the challenge is set to achieve the same or better result the following day. When we fall short, the drive is even stronger to improve. Day by day, week by week, this cycle drives us forward. Striving in this way sets the rhythm for the bakery. Piece by piece, tray by tray, attention is given to every step. The care that is dedicated to managing the precise temperatures, dough texture and every layer in the lamination is followed by the careful stretching and shaping of each piece. The morning baking team then brings the croissants to life with the same focus to every detail. The lamination is a strong example of our team's mentality and working style.

This collective respect, awareness and care for the details is at the core of Juno the Bakery. Each member of the team understands that their energy contributes to the quality of the end result, and their colleagues are all pushing in the same direction. From the mixing of the dough to forming the butter sheets, laminating, dividing, rolling, traying out, proving, egg washing, egg washing again, baking and packing. The acknowledgement that each piece will be cared for through its whole journey is a significant part of how we strive to keep the quality high.

Lamination
The lamination process is always delicate, challenging and relies largely on responding to changes in the dough, butter and temperature. Our guide, we hope, provides a starting point for laminating with or without a dough sheeter. The process takes a few days from mixing to baking the first croissant. Techniques detailed below can also be applied to the laminated brioche and puff pastry.

1, 2,

3, 4,

5, 6,

7, 8,

9, 10,

11, 12,

13, 14,

15, 16

CROISSANTS

Makes 10 pieces

Croissant dough (page 82)
1 block of rested laminated croissant dough

Egg wash
40g egg whites, 40g egg yolks, whisked

Follow the guide (page 82) and prepare the laminated dough.

Remove the rested laminated dough from the fridge (ensuring it is in the correct orientation) and begin rolling it out to approximately 5mm thick, 36cm high and 53cm long / 0.2 × 14.2 × 21in.

Place a ruler at the bottom of the dough. Starting on the left side, make a small mark with your knife on the bottom of the dough at 8cm / 3in increments. Move your ruler to the top of the piece. You will again mark in 8cm / 3in increments but will start at 4cm / 1.5in (i.e. 4cm, 12cm, 20cm / 1.5, 4.7, 8in etc.).

The following can be carried out with either a long and sharp chef's knife or with a ruler and a smaller blade.

If using a ruler, place the ruler so it hits the first mark on the bottom of the dough and the first mark on the top of the dough. Cut a clean, straight line. Keep the ruler on the same point at the top of the dough but move it to meet the second mark on the bottom of the dough. Cut one clean line. You should now have an isosceles triangle cut out (see photo guide).

Now, you will keep the bottom of the ruler in the same position and move the top to the second mark on the top of the dough. Cut your line, creating another triangle. Continue this pattern until you reach the end of the dough.

Place the triangles on a tray covered in cling film and return them to the fridge for their final rest. After about 30 minutes, take 2 pieces at a time out of the fridge and begin rolling out your croissants.

Croissant rolling
Take the base of the triangle in your left hand, with your 4 fingers at the back of the triangle and your thumb at the front. Using your right hand, gently grip the croissant directly under your left hand, again with your thumb at the front and fingers at the back. With a small amount of pressure, stretch the pointed part of the triangle downward until it is approximately 42cm / 16.5in in length. This may take more than once to do but the less times you handle your dough now the better your final result will be. Lay the triangle on the table in front of you with the base closest to your body and the point away from you.

Gently begin to roll the base of the triangle upward, using a back-and-forth motion at the beginning to get a tight roll, focusing on creating a tight roll at the start. Continue to push the base toward the tip, making sure to keep the piece as centred as possible. This will make for a nice and even shape of the croissant. Before finishing the roll, you can pick the croissant up in your hand and make sure that the tip or 'tail' is laying in the centre of the piece.

→

When traying up your croissants, place them far away enough from each other to allow them to roughly double in size. The 'tail' of the croissant at this point should be placed as close to the tray as possible without going underneath the croissant. Rest the croissants in the fridge until the following morning, alternatively prove and bake them on the same day.

Proving and baking
Prepare a baking tray lined with baking paper and tray out the croissants, leaving 4–5cm / 1.5–2in between each piece. Place each croissant on the tray, with the tallest part standing vertical, and in one motion pull open the tail of each croissant to release the tension.

Place them into a warm humid place and prove for about 2 hours until the layers begin to separate and the volume has increased by 30–40%.

After about 1.5 hours, preheat the oven to 200°C / 392°F on convection setting.

When the croissants are almost fully proved remove them from the humid place. Egg wash and allow to dry for 20 minutes. When dry and shiny, apply a second layer of egg wash, again allowing it to dry.

Place the croissants into the middle rack of the oven. Bake for 12 minutes, carefully turn the tray to ensure even baking and continue baking for another 5–7 minutes, until well caramelised.

Remove the croissants from the oven and allow them to cool.

PAIN AU CHOCOLAT

Makes 10 pieces

Croissant dough (page 82)
1 block of rested laminated croissant dough

Chocolate
160g dark chocolate, 70% cocoa, in batons, or tablets

Egg wash
40g egg whites, 40g egg yolks, whisked

Remove the rested laminated dough from the fridge and begin rolling it out to approximately 4.5mm thick, 40cm high and 40cm long / 0.18 × 15.7 × 15.7in. Each chocolate croissant will be 8cm / 3in wide and 20cm / 8in tall.

Place your ruler vertically along the dough and find the halfway point (20cm / 8in). Make small marks along the piece to ensure you get a straight line. Rotate your ruler horizontally and divide the dough length wise in two equal pieces, creating two rectangles, 20cm / 8in high and 40cm / 16in long.

Now take your ruler and place it along the bottom of the piece. Make markings at 8cm / 3in increments. Repeat at the top of the piece. Using your ruler to keep a straight line, cut vertically from the markings at the top to the markings at the bottom to get 8 × 20cm rectangles / 3 × 8in. Transfer the pieces to a tray with baking paper, cover with plastic and place in the fridge for 10 minutes.

Rolling
Lay out all of the pieces onto the table and place 1 chocolate baton or 2–3 tablets of chocolate at the top of each, leaving a 1mm / 0.04in gap of dough from the edge. Then one piece at a time, fold the top section with the chocolate down over itself and add the second chocolate baton (or tablets). Roll down to the end until the base of the rectangle is sitting to the side of the roll (as pictured). Cover tightly and store in the fridge overnight, or prove and bake right away.

Prepare a baking tray lined with baking paper and tray out the chocolate croissants, leaving 4–5cm / 1.5–2in between each piece. Place them in a warm humid place and prove for about 2 hours at 28°C / 82°F until the layers begin to separate and the volume has increased by 30–40% (see proving advice, page 32).

After about 1.5 hours, preheat the oven to 200°C / 392°F on convection setting.

When the chocolate croissants are almost fully proved, remove them from the humid place. Egg wash and allow to dry for 20 minutes. When dry and shiny, apply a second layer of egg wash, again allowing it to dry.

Place the chocolate croissants into the middle rack of the oven. Bake for 12 minutes, carefully turn the tray to ensure even baking and continue baking for another 5–7 minutes, until well caramelised.

Remove the croissants from the oven and allow them to cool.

ALMOND CROISSANTS

Makes 12–15 pieces

Croissant dough (page 82)
1 block of rested laminated croissant dough

Almond filling (page 330)
800g (560g inside, 240g for topping)

Almond flakes
400g

Citrus syrup (page 322)
100g in spray bottle

Prepare the almond filling and citrus syrup.

Remove the rested laminated dough from the fridge and begin rolling it out to a rectangle approximately 4.5mm thick and 36cm high / 0.18 × 14.2in. The exact length is not as important.

Using a pastry card, evenly spread the almond filling down the length of the dough, leaving a 2.5cm / 1in gap at the bottom edge. Starting from the top left corner of the dough, begin folding and crimping the dough along the top edge to create the beginning of a roll. Start again from the left corner and roll the dough down towards yourself, forming a tight spiral. You can gently pull the dough upwards while rolling to create more tension if needed. Roll the spiral down, finishing with the bottom edge, on the base of the roll.

Lightly dust the table and using the palms of your hands gently roll the tube up and down on the table to even it out. Return the roll to the fridge for 40 minutes to chill.

Remove the roll from the fridge and, using a large sharp knife, cut the roll into 12–15 rounds of 75–80g. After dividing the rounds, store them on a tray with baking paper, tightly wrapped in cling film. Let them rest in the fridge overnight.

Remove the almond croissants from the fridge. One at a time, take your round and grab the seam (piece of the dough with no almond filling on it). Pull lightly. Tuck this piece under the round. This will hold the almond croissant in place, or tray them out and prove and bake right away.

Place the rounds onto a baking tray lined with baking paper, with the seam still on the bottom. Leave 3–4cm / 1.2–1.5in between the pieces.

Proving
Place the tray in a warm humid place and prove at 28°C / 82°F for about 1.5 hours (see proving advice, page 32).

After 1 hour, preheat the oven to 190°C / 374°F on top and bottom heat setting.

When ready to bake, the spirals should have expanded by about 50% and the layers should start to separate.

→

Baking
Place the almond croissants into the oven on the middle rack. Bake for 5 minutes, turn the tray to ensure even baking and bake for 2–3 minutes more until even golden brown.

Remove the croissants from the oven and spray them with citrus syrup. If any of the spirals have spread too much, gently re-shape the spiral while hot. Allow to cool.

Leave the oven on for the next bake, raising the temperature to 205°C / 400°F on top and bottom heat setting.

Topping
Using a small plastic pastry scraper or palette knife, spread about 20g of almond filling onto the top of each almond croissant, covering the top of the spiral completely.

Next, place the almond flakes into a wide container that has enough space for the diameter of an almond croissant. Shake the box to align the flakes, continue shaking until most of the almond flakes are standing up. Take the almond croissant and in one firm movement press the surface with the almond filling into the flakes.

Place the croissant onto a tray lined with baking paper. Repeat with the remaining croissants, shaking the box as needed to align the flakes. Leave a space of 2cm / 0.8in between the pieces.

Second bake
Place the topped almond croissants back into the oven on the middle rack. Bake for 5 minutes, until the flakes are toasted and the filling is set.

Remove the almond croissants from the oven and spray them generously with the citrus syrup.

PISTACHIO CROISSANTS

Makes 12 pieces

Croissant dough (page 82)
1 block of rested laminated croissant dough

Pistachio filling (page 330)
560g

Rose syrup (page 324)
100g

Rum-soaked raisins
70g raisins
50g rum

Rose petals, dried
5–10g

Coarse ground pistachios
150g

Make the pistachio filling and rose syrup. Store each in an airtight container.

Soak the raisins in rum. Use a narrow container and cover completely to submerge the raisins. Soak overnight.

In a food processor, blitz the rose petals for just a few seconds until small flakes. Sieve them to remove the dust.

Blitz the pistachios, checking every 5 seconds or so, till broken into small chunks. It is important to not over-blend. Using a metal sieve, remove the finer pieces. These finer pieces can be blended further and be used in the pistachio filling.

Rolling
Drain the raisins completely and take the pistachio filing out of the fridge to warm up.

Remove the rested laminated dough from the fridge and begin rolling it out to approximately 4.5mm thick, 36cm high / 0.18 × 14.2in. The exact length is not as important.

Using a pastry card, evenly spread the pistachio filling down the length of the dough, leaving a 2.5cm / 1in gap at the bottom edge. Sprinkle the whole area covered with filling with the raisins.

Starting from the top left corner of the dough, begin folding and crimping the dough along the top edge to create the beginning of a roll. Start again from the left corner and roll the dough down towards yourself, forming a tight spiral. You can gently pull the dough upwards while rolling to create more tension if needed. Roll the spiral down, finishing with the bottom edge, on the base of the roll.

Lightly dust the table and, using the palms of your hands, gently roll the tube up and down on the table to even it out.

Wrap the roll tightly in plastic and return it to the fridge for 40 minutes to chill.

Remove the dough from the fridge and, using a large sharp knife, cut the roll into 12 rounds of 80–85g. After dividing the rounds, store them on a tray with baking paper and tightly covered in a plastic bag. Let them rest in the fridge overnight or tray them out and prove and bake right away.

→

50
KODAK PORTRA 800-2

Remove the pistachio croissants from the fridge. One at a time, take your rounds and grab the seam (piece of the dough with no pistachio filling on it). Pull lightly. Tuck this piece under the round. This will hold the pistachio croissant in shape.

Proving
Tray out the rounds onto a baking tray lined with baking paper, leaving 3–4cm / 1.2–1.5in between the pieces

Place the tray in a warm humid place and prove at 28°C / 82°F for about 1.5 hours (see proving advice, page 32).

After 1 hour, preheat the oven to 200°C / 392°F on top and bottom heat setting.

When ready to bake, the spirals should have expanded by about 50% and the layers should start to separate.

Baking
Place the croissants into the oven on the middle rack. Bake for 7 minutes, turn the tray to ensure even baking and bake for 4–5 minutes more until even golden brown.

Finishing
Remove the croissants from the oven and spray them with the rose syrup. If any of the spirals have spread too much, gently re-shape the spiral while hot. Then following the inside of the spiral where the filling is, place lines of the ground pistachios. Sprinkle with rose petals, then spray lightly with the rose syrup to keep the pistachios and petals in place.

RA 800-2
54
KODAK

TEBIRKES

Makes 10 pieces

Croissant dough (page 82)
1 block of rested laminated croissant dough

Tebirkes filling
20g glucose
55g white sugar
55g brown sugar
1g salt
95g extra fine almond flour
100g salted butter, soft

Egg wash
40g egg whites, 40g egg yolks, whisked

Poppyseeds
200g black poppyseeds

Prepare the filling and egg wash.

Tebirkes filling
Warm the glucose in the microwave to a pourable consistency.

In the bowl of a stand mixer with the paddle attachment, at slow speed mix together the white sugar, brown sugar, salt and almond flour. Mix until combined. Add the soft butter and mix until combined. Finally add the glucose and mix till combined. Transfer the filling to an airtight container.

Rolling
Remove the rested laminated dough from the fridge and begin rolling it out to approximately 4.5mm thick, 46cm high and about 40cm long / 0.18 × 18 × 15.7in.

Place your ruler vertically along the dough and find the halfway point (23cm / 9in). Make small marks at this height along the piece to ensure you get a straight line. Using a large sharp knife or razor blade, divide the dough lengthwise into two equal pieces, creating two rectangles, 23cm high and 40cm long / 9 × 15.7in.

Slightly warm up the tebirkes filling in a microwave till just above room temperature. Split the filling in two. In the top third of each piece, spread the filling in an even hump, about 7cm / 2.8in wide, from left to right. Egg wash the bottom 1cm / 0.4in along the length of the piece.

Now fold the top edge of the dough over the middle of the dough, leaving the bottom third uncovered. Bring the bottom third of the dough up over the centre section. The bottom edge should come half way over the centre of the piece to encase the filling. Grab either end of the piece and lift, stretching gently to even it out.

Transfer the two pieces onto a tray lined with baking paper, wrap tightly in plastic and allow to rest in the fridge for 30 minutes.

→

Dividing
Place the black poppyseeds into a wide container. Remove the pieces from the fridge and place them seam side up on a lightly floured surface. Roll each piece out until it is about 32cm / 12.5in long, ensuring it is an even thickness.

Lightly flour your bench and then flip over each piece. Egg wash the top and sides of the dough. Using a sharp large knife, cut each roll into 5 pieces, about 7cm / 2.8in wide and 10cm / 4in high, weighing 120–130g.

Transfer each piece into the black poppyseeds to coat the top and sides completely, avoiding poppyseeds sticking to the cut sides. Place the pieces on a tray lined with baking paper, wrap tightly in plastic and store in the fridge overnight, alternatively tray them out and prove and bake right away.

Baking
Prepare a baking tray lined with baking paper and tray out the tebirkes leaving 4–5cm / 1.5–2in between each piece.

Put them in a warm, humid place at 28°C / 82°F (see proving advice, page 32) and prove for about 2 hours, until the layers begin to separate and the volume has increased by 30–40%.

After about 1.5 hours, preheat the oven to 200°C / 392°F on convection setting.

When the tebirkes are almost fully proved, place the tray on the middle rack of the oven. Bake for 12 minutes, carefully turn the tray to ensure even baking and continue baking for another 5–7 minutes until well caramelised.

Remove the tebirkes from the oven and allow them to cool.

PAIN SUISSE WITH HAZELNUTS AND CHOCOLATE

Makes 8 pieces

Croissant dough (page 82)
1 block of rested laminated croissant dough

Rocher (page 292)
130g

Crème pâtissière (page 326)
100g

Citrus syrup (page 322)
100g

For the Pain Suisse with hazelnuts and chocolate, a cross-laminated croissant dough is used for a glass-light, extra crispy finish. Follow the lamination guide to the end, then follow the additional steps below to create the cross-lamination.

Day 1
Prepare the rocher without dipping in chocolate, the crème pâtissière and the citrus syrup.

Day 2
Place the crème pâtissière in a piping bag. Chop the rocher into small chunks around 2.5cm / 1in. Sieve the citrus syrup and transfer it to a spray bottle. The following steps can be used to make the cross laminated brioche (see page 122).

Remove the rested block of croissant dough from the fridge and, with the open end facing your body, roll it out horizontally to about 2cm / 0.8in thick.

Imagine the dough in two halves. The right half will be used to create the strips and the left half will be the base where the strips are layed down.

Lightly flour the right side of the dough. Brush the top of the left half with a small amount of water, just enough to make it sticky. Using a sharp knife or razor blade, slice 1mm / 0.04in thick vertical strips on the right side. Take each strip and place it with the layers facing up onto the wet section of the dough. Take care to make sure each strip is laid straight to ensure a clean finished result. Repeat this until the left side is entirely covered in strips.

Lightly flour the top of the dough. With a rolling pin, gently push over the exposed strips to ensure they are fully sealed to the base of the dough. Cover the dough tightly in plastic and rest it in the fridge for 30 minutes.

Dust the table in flour. Don't be afraid to be a bit heavy-handed here.

Remove the dough from the fridge. Flip over the piece with the strips down on the table and the open end of the dough piece again facing your body. Now roll the piece out horizontally to 4.5mm / 0.18in thick.

Avoid rolling upward as this will cause the strips to bulge and lose their definition.

→

Dividing
Cut away any scrap on the left side of the piece to make a straight line. Place a ruler at the base of the dough, with the straight line you just made being the start point. Make a mark along the bottom at 30cm / 12in increments. Repeat at the top of the dough. Cut a straight vertical line connecting the top markings to the bottom. Rotate each piece 90 degrees.

To check the dough is in the right orientation you can simply look under the piece and make sure the cross-laminated layers are pointing up.

Using your sharp knife, cut a thin straight line on the left side of the first piece. This opens up the layers to ensure you can see the beautiful lamination on the side when it bakes. Now, take your ruler and place it along the base of the first piece. Use the side you just cut as your starting point and make marks at 4.5cm / 1.8in intervals. Repeat on the top. Use your ruler to help you keep a straight line and cut vertical lines from the markings on top down to the bottom. Do this for both pieces.

As always with lamination, if the pieces are becoming too warm, place them on a tray, wrap them tightly and cool in the fridge for 15 minutes.

Filling
In the centre third of each strip, pipe a zig-zag line of crème pâtissière (12g), leaving a 1mm / 0.04in border on either side. Place roughly 16g of chopped rocher on top of the crème pâtissière. Fold the top section down and the bottom section up, so that the sides meet in the middle. Flip the piece over. Repeat with alle the pieces, place them on a tray, wrap it tightly in plastic and store it in the fridge.

Day 3
Prepare a baking tray lined with baking paper and tray out the pieces, leaving 4–5cm / 1.5–2in between each.

Put them into a warm, humid place at 28°C / 82°F (see proving advice, page 32) and prove for about 2 hours until the layers of the sides begin to separate and the volume has increased by 30–40%.

After about 1.5 hours, preheat the oven to 200°C / 392°F on the convection setting.

When fully proved, place the Pain Suisse with hazelnuts and chocolate on the middle rack of the oven. Bake for 12 minutes, carefully turn the tray to ensure even baking and continue baking for another 3–5 minutes, until golden brown.

Remove them from the oven and spray generously with the citrus syrup.

LAMINATED BRIOCHE DOUGH

Makes 980g dough

50g milk, 3.5% fat
210g eggs
125g salted butter
30g fresh yeast
500g white flour, 12% protein
60g white sugar
6g salt

Lamination butter sheet
450g salted butter

Mixing
Scale and chill all of the ingredients a few hours before mixing. In the bakery we store the flour in the freezer.

Add the milk, eggs, butter and yeast into the bowl of a stand mixer. Add the flour, sugar and salt. Using the dough hook attachment, mix for 10 minutes at slow speed, scrape the sides of the bowl. Mix another 2–3 minutes at medium speed. The dough should come together but still be rough in texture. With brioche dough for laminating, the dough should never reach full development. The lamination process will further add strength to the dough.

Remove the dough from the mixer. Shape it into a round ball. Using a bread knife, cut a cross about 1.5cm / 0.6in deep into the top of the dough. Press out the four corners to form a square. Use cling film to tightly wrap the dough and place the dough directly into the fridge at the coldest setting possible, 1–2°C / 34–36°F. Store the dough for 12–18 hours before starting the lamination process.

Lamination process (follow the croissant lamination guide on page 88, but with the measurements below)

Butter sheet
Prepare the butter sheet for the brioche to a 15 × 18cm / 6 × 7in rectangle.

Locking in the butter
Take the dough out of the fridge. Lightly flour the work surface and roll out the dough with firm even pressure until it is 1.5cm thick, 18cm wide and 27cm high / 0.6 × 7 × 10.6in. Follow the steps on page 82.

First double fold
Roll the dough to 7mm thick, 18cm high and 63cm long / 0.3 × 7 × 24.8in. Then follow the lamination guide for the double fold (page 85).

Second double fold
After resting, follow the same process again to complete a second double fold.

Resting
Wrap the dough tightly in cling film and rest in the fridge for a minimum of 1 hour to give the gluten in the dough a chance to relax. This will make the dough easier to work with and prevent it from ‘snapping back’ when you try to roll it out for the last time.

This dough can now be rolled out to different dimensions and be used for the other laminated products in the book.

CROSS-LAMINATED BRIOCHE DOUGH

(for blackcurrant and lavender buns)

Makes 12 pieces

Follow the same process as above with the laminated brioche, then follow the guide for cross-lamination, as show with the Pain Suisse with hazelnuts and chocolate recipe (page 114).

Remove the cross-laminated brioche dough from the fridge and roll out till the dough is 28cm / 11in high and 3mm / 0.1in thick. During this process, the cross-lamination side of the dough will be touching the table so make sure to use some flour to prevent sticking. The dough piece should be 28cm / 11in high, so trim the top and bottom of the dough accordingly.

Cut 3.5cm / 1.4in vertical strips. Take your left hand and place 3 fingers on the bottom section of the strip. This is to hold the band in place. Using your right hand, loop the strip around your fingers in a clockwise direction. Once you form a ring, take the piece in your right hand and tuck it under the bottom section that was being held by your left hand. The end result should be a ring with either end of the strip forming a base in the centre and the cross-lamination on the outside of the ring.

Place the rings on a tray, cover tightly with cling film and transfer to the fridge. (Follow the guide on page 182 included in the blackcurrant and lavender bun recipe).

Birke Filling

BUNS

CARDAMOM BUNS
CREAM BUNS
SAFFRON BUNS
VANILLA BUNS

Yeasted dough is the foundation of most of the pastries that originate from Scandinavia. If you have ever travelled through the Nordic countries, you most likely have noticed that you will not find a bakery without cardamom or cinnamon buns. When we opened the bakery, the cardamom bun was the very first item we knew we wanted to bake hence it became very important as we felt that it would act as a kind of lead singer. It led us to work tirelessly on perfecting yeasted dough and buns in different formats and flavours, particularly the cardamom bun. Yeasted dough for us needs to be soft, have the right amount of sweetness and be the main attraction, even when flavoured or filled. For Christmas we season the dough with an intense syrup made from the finest handpicked saffron. Saffron buns have their origin in Sweden and are a modern version of the traditional Lucia bun. The dough turns completely golden and has an incredible aroma. Buns in all shapes and flavours will always be a special part of the bakery. Especially the cardamom bun which has become a signature product. It is baked like all our other pastries throughout the whole day, so the chance to pick up a warm one is always there.

CARDAMOM BUNS

Makes 15–18 buns

Dough
15g green cardamom seeds
1000g white flour, 11% protein + extra for dusting
180g white sugar
5g fine sea salt
50g milk, 3.5% fat
400g water, cold
45g fresh yeast
220g salted butter, 5–12°C / 41–54°F

Butter filling (page 316)
460g butter filling

Cardamom sugar
30g green cardamom seeds
90g white sugar

Egg wash
2 whole eggs, beaten

Dough
Peel and coarsely crush the green cardamom seeds in a mortar and pestle or a spice grinder. Scale all the dry ingredients together into a bowl. Scale the milk, water, fresh yeast and butter cut into cubes into the bowl of a stand mixer with dough attachment. Mix everything together at slow speed for 15 minutes. Scrape the sides of the bowl and clear the hook. Resume mixing for 5 minutes at slow speed. Mix 1–2 minutes at second speed until the dough pulls away from the sides and is supple and elastic.

Prepare a baking sheet that can easily fit in the fridge. Lightly flour the baking sheet. Transfer the dough onto a lightly floured work surface. Dust the dough with flour. Fold the edges to the centre, forming a rectangle. Transfer the dough to the baking sheet. Wrap it tightly in plastic wrap or place it inside a large food safe plastic bag. Store the dough in the fridge overnight.

Butter filling
Cut the butter into small cubes in the bowl of a stand mixer. Scale the sugar and salt into the bowl. Mix butter, sugar and salt together at slow speed until just combined (2 minutes). Check that the mixture is evenly combined and if needed mix another 1 minute at slow speed. It's important to avoid overmixing. Transfer the filling to a microwave-safe plastic or glass container.

Cardamom sugar
Crack and coarsely crush the green cardamom seeds in a mortar and pestle or a spice grinder. Mix with the white sugar.

Egg wash
Crack and beat the eggs with a balloon whisk. Reserve in the fridge until use.

→

48
KODAK PORTRA 800-2

Rolling
Take the cardamom dough out of the fridge 20 minutes before starting to roll the buns. Lightly dust the work surface with flour. Transfer the dough from the baking sheet onto the table. Using a heavy rolling pin, roll the cardamom dough out to a rectangle 4mm / 0.2in thick, 70cm / 27.5in high and about 32cm / 12.5in wide.

Warm the butter filling in the microwave in 10 second intervals. It should be just above room temperature and soft but not melted or split. It is essential that the dough is about 12–15°C / 54–59°F before adding the butter filling.

When the dough and butter filling temperature are balanced, use a pastry card to transfer all of the butter filling onto the dough. Spread the filling evenly across the entire dough surface using a palette knife. Sprinkle about 30g of the cardamom sugar on top of the butter filling.

Mark the dough in thirds and fold the top third down and the bottom third up. Even out the edges and connect the right, left and top seams by pressing the dough together with your fingertips.

Dust the work surface with flour and lift the dough onto the floured area. Lightly dust the top of the folded dough with flour and begin rolling it out. The final dimensions should be 58cm / 22.8in long, 36cm / 14.2in high and 2.5cm / 1in thick. Using a pizza cutter and a thin dowel. Divide the dough into 90–100g strips, about 2.5cm / 1in wide and 36 / 14.2in high.

Shaping
Line a baking tray with baking paper. Pick up a strip and hold the end of the strip between the thumb and middle finger, with the longer end draped over the index finger. The laminated butter layers should be facing you.

With the right hand, take the long part of the strip, holding it close to the index finger, and bring the strip round the top of the middle and index fingers, forming an X-shape. Continue the motion and wrap the strip around again, placing the strip in between the X-shape.

Take the remaining slack, stretching gently, and bring the strip down and around to the thumb. Hold the strip in place with the thumb and bring the strip up and over the X. Make sure that the butter lamination is facing up and the strip is exactly in the centre of the bun. Tuck the end of the strip into the base of the bun.

Repeat with the remaining strips and place the finished buns onto the baking tray. Put the buns in a warm, humid place (see proving advice, page 32). It will take between 1 and 1.5 hours for the buns to rise, depending on the room temperature.

Baking
Preheat the oven to 215°C / 420°F, using the top and bottom heat setting with no fan. When the buns are ready gently egg wash them using a pastry brush. and place the baking sheet in the oven on the middle shelf. Bake for 7 minutes. Turn the tray carefully to ensure even baking. Bake the buns for another 4–5 minutes until they are golden brown.

Remove the buns from the oven and garnish each bun with a generous sprinkling of cardamom sugar.

CREAM BUNS

Makes 8 cream buns

Dough (page 130)
600g cardamom dough

These light, sweet buns with hints of cardamom provide the perfect base for our semlor and seasonal cream buns. They are also great on their own, enjoyed warm from the oven with a bit of butter.

Shaping
Remove the cardamom dough from the fridge and divide it into 60g pieces. Now roll these into round buns and transfer the buns to a baking tray lined with baking paper, leaving 5cm / 2in between them.

Place the buns in a warm, humid place, 28–30°C / 82–86°F (see proving advice, page 32). It will take between 2 and 2.5 hours for the buns to rise (depending on the exact temperature). It is important that they rise to the maximum size. This is only possible if you avoid skin from forming on the surface. A water misting bottle can be used during the rising process.

Baking
Preheat the oven to 200°C / 392°F using the convection setting.

When the buns are fully proved, place them in the oven on the middle rack. Bake with steam pans (see page 32) for 8 minutes, then turn the tray for even baking and check the buns. Add 2–3 minutes if necessary. Bake the buns until they are evenly golden brown.

Remove the buns from the oven and carefully transfer them to a cooling rack. Allow them to cool for 30–35 minutes before using for flavoured cream buns or semlor.

SAFFRON BUNS

Makes 15–18 buns

Saffron syrup
3g saffron
10g cognac
45g water
55g white sugar
5g glucose

Dough
1000g white flour, 11% protein
160g white sugar
8g fine sea salt
225g salted butter, 5–12°C / 41–54°F
420g water, cold
45g saffron syrup, cold
45g milk, 3.5% fat
45g fresh yeast

Butter filling (page 316)
460g butter filling

Egg wash
2 whole eggs, beaten

Topping
100g pearl sugar

Saffron syrup
Two days before preparing the dough, make the saffron syrup. Macerate the saffron in the cognac and leave it in the fridge for 24 hours. Bring water, glucose and sugar to a boil. Cool the syrup to room temperature and gently stir in the cognac-saffron mix.

Dough and butter filling
Follow the same procedure as for the cardamom buns (see page 130). Add the saffron syrup. Omit the cardamom sugar topping both in the lamination and on the buns after baking. Eggwash the buns before baking, and after baking garnish with a sprinkling of pearl sugar.

ODAK PORTRA 800-2
46
M ---- 1/60
AE-5.0 A
199

VANILLA BUNS

Makes 18 buns

Dough
2kg cardamom dough without cardamom (page 130)

Vanilla filling
280g salted butter, 12°C / 54°F
160g white sugar
60g vanilla sugar
3g fine sea salt

Rum crème pâtissière
200g crème pâtissière (page 326)
5g dark rum

Vanilla syrup (page 320)
50g in spray bottle

Day 1

Dough
Follow the same base recipe as for the cardamom dough (page 130), omitting the cardamom from the recipe. The procedure is the same until the rolling and shaping stage of the process. For the vanilla buns, prepare the vanilla filling, vanilla syrup and rum crème pâtissière.

Vanilla filling
At slow speed in a stand mixer using the paddle attachment, gently mix the butter, sugar, vanilla sugar and salt. Mix until just combined. Store at room temperature, best between 24–28°C / 75–82°F.

Rum crème pâtissière
Whisk crème pâtissière and dark rum together till velvety smooth, but not runny. Transfer to a piping bag and reserve in the fridge.

Day 2

Rolling
Take the dough out of the fridge 20 minutes before starting to roll the buns. Lightly dust the work surface with flour. Transfer the dough from the baking sheet onto the table. Using a heavy rolling pin, roll the dough out to a rectangle 6.5cm thick, 55cm high and about 30cm wide / 2.5 × 21.5 × 12in.

Warm the butter filling in the microwave in 10 second intervals. It should be just above room temperature and soft but not melted or split. It is essential that the dough is about 12–15°C / 54–59°F before adding the butter filling.

When the dough and filling temperature is perfect, transfer all of the vanilla filling onto the dough and spread it evenly across the entire surface. Mark the dough in thirds and fold the top third down and the bottom third up. Even out the edges and connect the right, left and top seams by pressing the dough together with your fingertips.

Dust the work surface with flour and lift the dough onto the floured area. Lightly dust the top of the folded dough and begin rolling it out, taking time in between for the dough to relax between movements with the rolling pin.

The final dimensions should be 1.5cm thick, 32cm high and 55cm long / 0.6 × 12.5 × 21.5in. Using a pizza cutter and a thin dowel, divide the dough into 18 strips about 95–105g. Each strip should measure about 2.5 × 32cm / 1 × 12.5in.

→

Shaping
Take a strip and rotate it 90 degrees without twisting, so that the layers are facing up. Starting at one end, gently rotate the strip around itself, forming a coil. Tuck the end of the strip under the centre of the coil. If the weight needs to be adjusted, pinch off a piece of the end of the strip or add a bit of dough underneath the coil at the end of shaping.The final roll should be about 7.5–8cm / 3in in diameter. Transfer the shaped buns to a baking tray lined with baking paper. Leave 4–5 cm / 2in between the buns.

Put the tray in a warm, humid place at 28–30°C / 82–86°F (see proving advice, page 32). It will take between 1 and 1.5 hours for the buns to rise, depending on the room temperature.

Baking
Preheat the oven to 205°C / 400°F, using the top and bottom heat setting with no fan. When the buns are fully proved, press down the centre of each spiral, using two fingers lightly dipped in cold water. Pipe about 20g of rum crème pâtissière into each bun.

Place the baking sheet in the oven on the middle rack. Bake the buns for 7 minutes, then turn the tray carefully to ensure even baking. Bake for another 4–5 minutes until the buns are golden brown.

Remove the baking sheet from the oven and generously spray the buns with the vanilla syrup.

WINTER

LEMON CAKE
LEMON CREAM BUNS
SEMLOR
DANISH CARNIVAL BUNS
CHOCOLATE TARTS

The new year at the bakery always begins with a true winter highlight from Sweden, semlor: soft cardamom-scented buns filled with almond paste and whipped cream. The cream – whipped just to soft peaks and not too stiff – folds naturally on top of the buns when piped, making them pure indulgence. Semlor are a classic part of Carnival season which acts as a bright and festive period during the often cold and grey winter months. In this period bakeries explode with buns in a multitude of flavours, one more irresistible than the other. Lemons are at their very best this time of year, and we use them to make lemon cream buns and our lemon cake: a simple, yet refined and tender cake that has become a true house favourite. Winter is the perfect season for chocolate, and our chocolate tart is a testament to our long-term relationship with Mikkel Friis-Holm, who makes chocolate of the most exceptional quality just 40 minutes away from the bakery.

LEMON CAKE

Makes one 500g cake

Batter
20g lemon juice (approximately half of 1 lemon)
Zest of 1 lemon
100g extra fine almond flour
180g white sugar
2g salt
110g salted butter, room temperature
135g eggs
85g white flour, 11% protein
4g baking powder

Lemon syrup
20g water
15g lemon juice
20g white sugar

Lemon sugar
Zest of 2 lemons
200g white sugar

Preheat the oven to 160°C / 320°F on the top and bottom heat setting. Grease a baking tin, 10cm deep, 10cm wide, 18cm long / 4 × 4 × 7in, cut baking paper to the size of the tin and line it with the paper.

Batter
Juice the lemon and peel the zest. Scale the ingredients and sift the flour. Place the almond flour, sugar and salt into the bowl of a stand mixer with the paddle attachment and mix until combined. Add the butter to the mixture one third at a time and mix at slow speed until combined. Scrape down the edges of the bowl using a pastry card. Then add the lemon juice and zest and begin adding the eggs gradually until combined. Scrape down the sides. Add the flour and the baking powder. Mix until just combined. Gently transfer the batter into the lined baking tin.

Baking
Place the tin in the oven on the middle rack. Bake the cake for 45 minutes.

Allow the cake to cool for 20–30 minutes. While the cake is cooling down, prepare the lemon syrup.

Lemon syrup
Bring all ingredients to the boil in a saucepan, then remove it from the heat and leave to cool.

Lemon sugar
In a large container, wide enough to fit the whole cake, zest the lemons and blend well with the sugar.

Glazing
Carefully remove the cake from the tin and place it on a tray. While the cake is still warm, use a pastry brush to gently distribute the lemon syrup onto all sides of the cake, making sure all the syrup is absorbed into the cake.

Finishing
When the cake is completely cool (it takes at least 2–3 hours), lift it into the lemon sugar and coat all surfaces with the sugar.

LEMON CREAM BUNS

Makes 8 buns

Buns
8 baked buns (page 130)

Filling
450g diplomat cream (page 328)
300g lemon curd

Lemon curd
70g salted butter
40g lemon juice
100g white sugar
90g eggs
1 gelatine leaf, soaked in cold water

Garnish
30g salted butter, melted
200g white sugar
Zest of 1 lemon, julienned

Day 1
The day before you would like to serve the lemon cream buns, prepare the cardamom dough (page 130), lemon curd and crème pâtissière for the diplomat cream (page 328). The diplomat cream is mixed shortly before piping for the best consistency.

Lemon curd
Juice the lemons. Melt butter, lemon juice and sugar in a pan to 50°C / 122°F. Add the eggs gradually in order not to curdle them. Whisk consistently and bring the mixture to 80°C / 176°F. Whisk in gelatine and pass the mixture through a sieve. Leave it to set for at least 6 hours in the fridge.

Day 2
Roll, prove and bake 8 cream buns (see page 140).

While the cream buns are cooling down, prepare about 450g of diplomat cream (page 328).

Filling and garnishing
Use a sharp knife to poke a small hole in the base of each bun. Transfer the lemon curd to a piping bag and pipe about 35g into each bun.

Using another piping bag, insert a 13mm / 0.5in nozzle and fill the bag with the diplomat cream. Pipe about 35–40g diplomat cream into each bun. Use a pastry scraper to remove any excess filling.

Melt the butter and evenly brush each bun. Allow the butter to set for a few minutes.

Transfer each bun into a bowl with the white sugar and coat them completely. Move the buns to a presentation tray and pipe a small spire of diplomat cream on top. Garnish with two strips of lemon zest.

SEMLOR

Makes 8 buns

Buns
480g cardamom dough (page 130)

Filling
125g marzipan, 66% almond, 34% sugar
125g ground almonds
2 drops of almond essence
1g salt
30g vanilla syrup (page 320)
95g cream, 38% fat

Topping
100g Valencia almonds
300g cream, 38% fat
50g icing sugar

Prepare the cardamom dough (page 130), vanilla syrup (page 320), and filling.

Filling
In the bowl of a stand mixer using the paddle attachment, mix the marzipan, ground almonds, salt and almond essence until a crumbly consistency. Gradually add the vanilla syrup, then add the cream gradually until it becomes a paste. Transfer the filling to a piping bag and let it rest in the fridge for at least 2 hours.

Buns
Roll, prove and bake 8 buns (see page 140). After baking the buns, cool the oven to 150°C / 302°F for the almonds.

While the buns are cooling down, spread the almonds on a baking tray lined with baking paper and roast them, checking every 3–4 minutes, until evenly roasted. Chop the almonds and finally whip the cream.

Remove the filling from the fridge about 30 minutes before piping.

Assembly
Using a sharp bread knife, slice the top third off the top of the cream buns, this piece will be used as the lid of each bun. With sharp scissors, trim the edges of each lid to create a 6cm / 2.4in round.

Pipe about 45g of filling onto the base of each bun, then scatter 12g of the toasted almonds evenly on top.

In the bowl of a stand mixer using the whisk attachment, whip the cream till just before soft peaks, then, using a metal whisk, finish whipping by hand. The cream should be a velvety texture. Transfer the cream to a piping bag with a metal 5mm / 0.2in fluted nozzle and pipe a swirl coming up from the base of the filling, about 5cm / 2in high. Place the lid on top of the cream.

Lightly dust the tops of the buns with icing sugar.

DANISH CARNIVAL BUNS

Makes 12–15 pieces

Brioche (page 120)
1 block laminated brioche dough

Our carnival buns are based on laminated brioche dough. For the banana caramel and chocolate buns, we use rolls of laminated brioche caramelised in raw cane sugar and baked in fluted brioche tins. For the blackcurrant lavender buns, a cross-laminated version of our brioche dough suits the purpose best. See our lamination guide (page 88).

CHOCOLATE AND VANILLA BUNS

Makes 12 buns

Brioche baskets
1 block rested laminated brioche dough (page 120)
30g salted butter, melted
200g raw cane sugar

Vanilla crème pâtissière
460g crème pâtissière (page 326)
1 vanilla pod, scraped
(prepare 460g in total, 180g of this is for the diplomat cream)

Whipped chocolate ganache
60g dark chocolate, 60% cocoa, chopped
85g cream, 38% fat
5g glucose
5g honey
1g gelatine, soaked in cold water
105g cream, 38% fat, cold

Chocolate discs
100g dark chocolate, 60% cocoa, tempered (page 336)

Diplomat cream (page 328)
360g

Chopped chocolate
60g dark chocolate, 60% cocoa

Garnish
50g cocoa powder
Few pinches of sea salt flakes

Preparation

Day 1

Brioche baskets
Remove the rested laminated brioche dough from the fridge. Roll the dough down to a 3.5mm thick, 26.5cm high and 50cm long sheet / 0.15 × 10.4 × 19.7in. Measure the whole sheet into 3.5cm sections, 26.5cm high / 1.4 × 10.4in.

Using the tip of a sharp knife or razor blade, cut the dough into strips following the measurements. Roll each strip up into a coil, making sure that the rolls are even on the top and bottom sides of the spiral. Transfer the rolls to a tray, wrap them in plastic and store in the fridge.

Vanilla crème pâtissière
Prepare the crème pâtissière that will be required for the diplomat cream. For this recipe we increase the amount of vanilla in the cream. Reserve it in the fridge.

Whipped chocolate ganache
Chop the chocolate into small pieces and place them in a heat-proof mixing bowl. Heat the cream, glucose and honey in a saucepan until steaming. Pour the cream over the chocolate and let it melt the chocolate for 1–2 minutes. Gently mix with a spatula. Add the gelatine and mix gently. Finally add the cold cream. Allow the ganache to cool and transfer it to an airtight container. Store it in the fridge to set overnight.

Chocolate discs
For the top of the bun, we use a round disc of tempered chocolate. On a tray lined with baking paper, place an acetate plastic strip. Mark out 12 circles, each 5cm / 2in in diameter, on the acetate, leaving about 1.5cm / 0.6in between them. Prepare a second sheet of acetate in the same size, but without marking; this will be used to form the chocolate disc.

Temper 100g chocolate (page 336). Transfer it to a piping bag and pipe about 5g of chocolate into the centre of each circle on the acetate plastic. After piping, place the other acetate sheet on top and press lightly with a flat edge, so the chocolate spreads to the border of each circle. Allow the discs to set at room temperature. Once they are set, remove the chocolate discs from the acetate and transfer them to a tray with baking paper.

→

Day 2

Brioche
Using cooking oil spray, thoroughly spray 12 fluted coated aluminium brioche tins, 4cm high × 11cm diameter / 1.6 × 4.4in. Take the rolls of laminated brioche and brush each brioche with melted butter to coat completely. Toss each roll in raw cane sugar. Place them into the fluted tins.

Proving and baking
Place the brioche rolls in a warm, humid place. It will take about 2.5 hours for the brioche to rise at about 28°C / 82°F (see proving guide, page 32).

When the brioches have risen and are soft to the touch, and the layers are separating, preheat the oven to 170°C / 338°F on the convection setting.

Prove until the top of the brioches only gently bounces back when pressed. It is important to prove them quite far to achieve the lightest result. When the brioche rolls are fully proved, use a 4.5cm diameter and 4.5cm high / 1.8 × 1.8in canelé tin or other metal insert of a similar size. Press a canelé tin down into the centre of each brioche, about 40% of the way down. When all the canelé tins are in place, transfer the brioches to the oven on the middle rack.

Bake the brioches for about 17 minutes. Turn the tray halfway through baking to evenly colour the brioches.

Remove the brioches from the oven. If the dough has lifted the canelé tins up significantly, gently press them back down.

Remove each brioche from its tin. The cooler they become, the harder it will be. If they stick, return them to the oven one or two at a time, warm for a minute or two, then try again to turn them out of the tins. If necessary, take a knife and run it around the edge of the fluted tin to release the dough.

Allow the brioche to cool.

→

Whipped ganache
In the bowl of a stand mixer using the whisk attachment, whisk the ganache at medium speed for 20 seconds, scrape down the sides of the bowl and mix again for 10 seconds until lightly mixed. Transfer the ganache to a piping bag.

Diplomat cream
Mix the diplomat cream and transfer it to a piping bag with a 13mm / 0.5in round nozzle.

Assembly
When the brioche is completely cool, begin assembling the buns. Dust the chocolate discs generously with cocoa powder.

The following can be done step by step for each of the 12 buns: Pipe 25g of crème pâtissière into the base. Pipe about 20g of the whipped ganache on top. Add 5g of chopped chocolate. Add a few flakes of sea salt. With 30g of diplomat cream, pipe a wide dome to about 1cm / 0.4in above the rim of the brioche. Finally place a cocoa-dusted chocolate disc on top.

BANANA AND CARAMEL BUNS

Makes 12 buns

Brioche baskets
12 laminated brioche baskets (page 174)
Cooking oil spray
20g salted butter, melted
200g raw cane sugar

Diplomat cream (page 328)
300g

Rum caramel
75g water
250g white sugar
250g cream, 38% fat
¼ of a vanilla pod, scraped
50g salted butter
125g rum
2g salt

Banana puree
3 large ripe bananas
Salt

Chocolate
100g dark chocolate, 60% cocoa

Banana garnish
1 banana
20g raw cane sugar

Prepare the crème pâtissière that will be required for the diplomat cream (page 326).

Brioche baskets
Follow the steps for shaping, proving and baking the brioche baskets as shown in the chocolate and vanilla recipe (page 174).

Rum caramel
In a heavy-based pan, start with the water and swirl the pan slightly to coat the base. Add the sugar and slowly heat on medium until the caramel is 180°C / 356°F. Avoid stirring as that can cause the caramel to crystallize. Take the pan off the heat.

In a separate pot, warm the cream and vanilla seeds together. Pour the warmed cream into the caramel and stir together. Place the mixture back onto the heat and bring it to 108°C / 226°F. Take the pan off the heat and add the butter. Finally, stir in the rum and salt.

Leave the mixture to set and cool, then transfer to a piping bag. Store at room temperature to prevent crystallisation.

Banana puree
Scale the weight of the three peeled bananas and add 1% of their weight in salt. Blitz the bananas with salt in a food processor until puree consistency.

Chocolate
Chop it into thin shards.

Diplomat cream (page 328)
Transfer it to a piping bag with a 13mm / 0.5in metal nozzle.

Banana garnish
Slice the banana into 1cm / 0.4in thick coins. Add raw cane sugar on top and caramelise using a blowtorch.

Assembly
For each brioche:
Spoon 14g banana puree into the base of the brioche followed by piping 20g of the rum caramel in a spiral motion on top of the puree. Add about 8g of chopped chocolate. Pipe the diplomat cream in an upwards motion with even pressure to fill the hole and create a round top. Finish by adding the caramelised banana coins in the centre.

BLACKCURRANT AND LAVENDER BUNS

Makes 12 buns

Brioche (page 174)
12 cross-laminated brioches

Vanilla syrup (page 320)
90g vanilla syrup

Marzipan cream
85g marzipan, 66% almond, 34% sugar
34g extra fine almond flour
50g vanilla syrup (page 320)
70g crème pâtissière (page 326)

Blackcurrant jam
120g blackcurrant puree
25g white sugar

Lavender sugar
1g dried lavender blossoms
30g white sugar

Macerated blackcurrants
150g blackcurrants
30g lavender sugar

Diplomat cream (page 328)
550g

Day 1 *(the day before baking the brioche, same day as finishing lamination)*

Crème pâtissière
Prepare the crème pâtissière that will be required for the diplomat cream (page 326) and for the marzipan cream.

Blackcurrant jam
Put the blackcurrant puree and sugar in a pan on medium heat. Reduce for 5–6 minutes, stirring occasionally.

Vanilla syrup
Prepare a batch of vanilla syrup and allow it to infuse overnight (page 320).

Lavender sugar
In a spice grinder, blitz the lavender blossoms (reserve a few for decoration). Mix with the sugar and leave to infuse overnight.

Macerated blackcurrants
Toss the blackcurrants with the lavender sugar till the berries are completely coated. Store in the fridge.

Day 2

Marzipan cream
In the bowl of a stand mixer with paddle attachment, mix the marzipan and the almond flour at slow speed until it has a crumbly texture. Add the vanilla syrup and mix until smooth.

In a mixing bowl, whisk the crème pâtissière to remove any lumps. Add it to the mixer bowl and mix until combined. Transfer the marzipan cream into a piping bag and set aside.

Diplomat cream (page 328)
Prepare and transfer to a piping bag with a 16mm / 0.6in metal nozzle.

Proving and baking
Tray out 12 pieces of cross-laminated brioche onto a large baking tray lined with baking paper, leaving 3–4cm / 1–1.5in between the pieces. Place in a warm humid place and prove for about 1.5 to 2 hours at 28°C / 82°F (see proving advice, page 32).

After about 1 hour, preheat the oven to 190°C / 374°F on the top and bottom heat setting.

→

Check the proving, the centre of each piece should have risen and be soft and airy to touch. Using a small bowl with cold water, dip your index and middle fingers into the water. With wet fingers, press out the centre of each brioche, degassing, flattening and gently expanding the centre to create space for the marzipan cream.

After pressing, pipe 20g of marzipan cream into each brioche.

Put the tray in the oven on the middle rack. While the brioches are baking, transfer the remaining vanilla syrup to a spray bottle.

Bake the brioches for 6 minutes, turn the tray to evenly colour the brioche and continue baking for another 4 minutes. Check the colouration and add 2–3 minutes until each piece is an even golden brown.

Remove the brioches from the oven and spray generously with the vanilla syrup. Allow them to cool.

Assembly
For each of the buns:
Pipe 10g of blackcurrant jam into the centre. On top of the jam, pipe a single generous dome of diplomat cream, about 45g. Using the back of a spoon, in one motion create a wide well on top of the cream. Place about 15g of macerated blackcurrants into the well. Decorate with a few lavender blossoms.

CHOCOLATE TARTS

Makes 8 tarts

Chocolate sablé
125g salted butter, soft
90g icing sugar
50g eggs
250g white flour, 11% protein
30g extra fine ground almond flour
30g cocoa powder
2g salt

Ganache
250g dark chocolate, 70% cocoa
300g cream, 38% fat
75g glucose
25g salted butter, room temperature

Garnish
5g flakey salt

Grease 8 perforated tart tins, 2cm high, 7cm in diameter / 0.8 × 2.8in. Set them aside till later.

Mixing
In the bowl of a stand mixer, mix the butter and icing sugar until combined. Add the eggs gradually while on low speed. Finally, add the flour, almond flour, cocoa powder and salt. Mix until combined and homogeneous.

Place the dough on a floured tabletop and knead to get rid of any residual lumps. Split the dough into two pieces, a piece of 430g and a smaller one of 130g. Wrap each piece in cling film and let it rest in the fridge for 2 hours.

After resting, remove the small piece from the fridge and use a rolling pin to roll the dough out to a rectangle 2.5mm / 1in thick. Carefully transfer the rolled-out dough to a baking tray and place the dough in the fridge. Repeat with the large piece.

One by one, remove the two doughs from the fridge and with firm pressure roll the spiked docking roller over the dough. Then return the doughs to the fridge.

Once the smaller sheeted dough is cold, push the tart tins into the dough, ensuring the dough sticks to the base of the tins. If the dough is raised, push the centre of the dough down slightly to ensure a flat base.

Remove the larger piece of dough from the fridge and on a lightly floured surface, using a sharp knife and a ruler, cut the dough into strips of 2cm height and 21cm length / 0.8 × 8in.

Lining
Line the strips around the edges of the tart tins, making sure there is a good connection at the ends and to the base. Using your thumbs, gently press into the edges to ensure the connection between the strip and the base.

→

©2022

Baking
Preheat your oven to 180°C / 356°F on fan setting.

Place the tarts in the fridge for about 10 minutes to harden, then remove them from the fridge and, using a small sharp knife, trim the top edges in line with the tart rings. Transfer the tart tins to a baking tray and place it on the middle rack of the oven. Bake them for 9 minutes.

Leave the baked tart shells to cool completely before carefully removing them from the rings.

Ganache
Chop the chocolate into small pieces and place them in a heat-proof mixing bowl. Heat the cream and glucose in a saucepan until steaming. Pour the cream over the chocolate and let it melt the chocolate for 1–2 minutes. Add the butter and gently mix with a spatula. The mix should be shiny and glossy. Allow it to cool slightly and transfer the ganache to a small jug with a pouring spout.

Assembly
Slowly pour 50g of the chocolate ganache into each tart shell. Place the shells in the fridge to set for 20 minutes. Add a pinch of sea salt in the centre of each tart to finish.

For the best texture, remove the tarts from the fridge 20 minutes or more before serving.

SPRING

RHUBARB AND ELDERFLOWER TART
RHUBARB AND PISTACHIO FRANGIPANE TARTS
RHUBARB BUNS
MILK SLICES
OTHELLO CAKES

After many cold months, spring arrives gently with new energy. With this season comes rhubarb. A vivid ingredient full of freshness and acidity. The rhubarb and pistachio frangipane was one of our first creations back in 2018 and still features every year at the bakery. The richness of crushed pistachio kernels paired with the bright flavours of the rhubarb is a perfect match. Last spring we created a new rhubarb tart focused entirely on rhubarb. Slices of slowly baked rhubarb covered in elderflower jelly. Underneath hides the freshest lime-scented rhubarb compote, all wrapped in a brittle tart. The feeling of spring in one bite. The classics, Othello and milk slice, act as a bridge between the seasons, bringing both comfort and a sense of lightness that often feels needed this time of year. The milk slice, a sweet slice of childhood memories for many, is familiar yet refreshed with the addition of soft milk caramel.

RHUBARB AND ELDERFLOWER TART

Makes one tart

Sablé
30g extra fine-ground almonds
250g white flour, 11% protein
95g icing sugar
2g salt
175g salted butter
50g eggs

Blind baking
300g white rice or baking beads

Rhubarb compote
375g rhubarb stalks
185g white sugar

Rhubarb slices
2 thick rhubarb stalks with a nice red colour
200g white sugar, for coating the stalks in a wide container

Elderflower jelly
100g elderflower syrup
2 gelatine leaves, soaked in cold water

Lime-rhubarb compote mix
230g rhubarb compote (from above)
30g raw rhubarb brunoise
2g lime zest
6g lime juice

Garnish
1 lime to zest

Prepare the sablé, rhubarb compote, rhubarb slices and elderflower jelly.

Sablé
Add the ground almonds into the bowl of a stand mixer with the paddle attachment. Sieve in the rest of the dry ingredients and mix until combined. Add the softened butter and mix to a crumbly consistency. Add the eggs gradually while on low speed. Mix until just combined. Place the dough onto a floured tabletop and knead to get rid of any remaining lumps. Wrap the dough in cling film and let it rest in the fridge for at least 2 hours or overnight.

Rhubarb compote
Wash and chop the rhubarb stalks into large pieces, 3–5cm / 1.2–2in. Place the rhubarb and sugar into a pot on medium heat. Cook for 10–15 minutes while stirring occasionally to prevent the compote from sticking to the base of the pan. Cook until the compote is thickened and glossy. Transfer it to an airtight container and cover the surface with cling film to prevent skin from forming. Reserve the compote in the fridge.

Rhubarb slices
Preheat the oven to 160°C / 320°F on top and bottom heat setting. Line a baking sheet with baking paper.

Peel the rhubarb stalks and keep the skins in a separate container as they will be used later for the elderflower syrup. Cut each stalk so they are 14cm / 5.5in in length. Using a mandolin, slice along the length of each stalk into 5mm / 0.2in thick slices. Gently toss the slices in white sugar to coat.

Place each strip, flesh-side down, on a baking tray, arranging the strips with a little space between. Transfer the tray to the middle rack in the oven. Bake the strips just until they are soft. Check after 5 minutes, continue baking 2–3 minutes until the rhubarb can just be pierced with the tip of a sharp knife. Remove the strips from the oven, allow them to cool and transfer them to the fridge.

Grease a fluted aluminium tart mould with removable base, 35cm long × 11cm wide, 2.5cm deep / 14 × 4.4 × 1in. Preheat the oven to 170°C / 338°F on convection setting.

Remove the sablé from the fridge, place it on a floured tabletop and, using a rolling pin, roll to a 2.5mm / 0.1in thick rectangle, about 42cm / 16.5in long, 27cm / 10.6in wide. Using a sharp knife, cut the sablé to 40cm / 15.7in long and 17cm / 6.7in wide. Return the sablé to the fridge for 15–20 minutes.

→

Carefully lift the sablé sheet into the mould and line the mould by gently pressing the sablé into the fluted edges, making sure there are no air gaps. Let the sablé rest in the fridge for at least 30 minutes.

Line the inside of the tart shell with heat-proof plastic wrap, making sure to keep about 5cm / 2in of excess cling film on all sides. Fill with white rice or baking beads, then gently fold the excess cling film over the centre. Transfer the mould to the middle rack of the oven and blind bake for 25 minutes.

After this, remove the rice (or beads) and plastic wrap and continue baking for another 5–8 minutes until the tart shell is golden and evenly baked. Remove from the oven and allow it to cool before turning the shell out of the mould.

Lime-rhubarb compote mix
Wash and chop the fresh rhubarb to a fine brunoise. Using a large spoon or silicone spatula, fold the chopped raw rhubarb, lime juice and zest into the cooked compote. Reserve the mixture in the fridge.

Elderflower jelly
Boil the elderflower syrup with the rhubarb skins until the rhubarb skin colour bleeds into the syrup. Remove the pot from the heat and add the gelatine.

Assembly
Place the rhubarb-lime compote mix into the tart base and spread in an even layer. Trim the sheet of baked rhubarb slices to 10cm / 4in in length and place on top of the compote layer with the flesh side up, creating a single layer of rhubarb slices.

Store the tart in the fridge for 15 minutes.

Warm the elderflower jelly to a pourable consistency. Pour it into a piston funnel or a piping bag (take care as it will be hot). Slowly pour the jelly over the surface of the rhubarb strips to create an even layer. Take care not to work too fast here as you may create bubbles in the jelly. Return the tart to the fridge for 20 minutes to set the jelly.

Once the jelly sets, garnish the top of the tart with lime zest and cut it into about 6 slices.

RHUBARB AND PISTACHIO FRANGIPANE TARTS

Makes 10 tarts

5–6 stalks of rhubarb
Sablé for 10 tarts (page 332)
350g pistachio frangipane in piping bag (page 334)
Icing sugar for dusting, if needed

Frangipane and sablé
Prepare the sablé (page 332) and the pistachio frangipane (page 334) and line ten 8cm / 3in tart tins, with the sablé.

Rhubarb
Wash the rhubarb stalks and cut them into 1cm / 0.4in pieces, depending on the thickness. Each tart will be best with 5 pieces per tart, standing skin side up.

Preheat the oven to 190°C / 374°F on the top and bottom heat setting.

Finishing
Pipe about 35g of pistachio frangipane into each tart. Then place about 5 pieces of cut rhubarb in the frangipane, pressing gently.

Baking
Transfer the tarts to a heavy baking tray and place it on the centre rack of the oven. Bake for about 17 minutes, carefully turning the tray halfway through to ensure even baking.

Remove the tarts from the oven and leave them to cool slightly before removing them from the tins.

When they are cool, taste one of the tarts and if the acidity of the rhubarb is too strong, lightly dust the tarts with icing sugar.

RHUBARB BUNS

Makes 16–18 buns

Buns
One batch of vanilla buns (page 152)

Vanilla syrup (page 320)
90g vanilla syrup

Filling
200g créme pâtissière (page 326)

Rhubarb compote
375g rhubarb
185g white sugar

Follow the vanilla bun recipe (page 152) and prepare the vanilla syrup, the créme pâtissière (page 326) and the rhubarb compote.

Rhubarb compote
Wash and chop the rhubarb stalks into large pieces, 3–5cm / 1.2–2in. Place the rhubarb and sugar into a pot on medium heat. Cook for 10–15 minutes while stirring occasionally to prevent the compote from sticking to the base of the pan. Cook until the compote is thickened and glossy, allow it to cool completely and transfer to a piping bag.

Follow the same proving and baking procedure as shown in the vanilla bun recipe (page 152), except pipe about 10g of créme pâtissière into each bun, followed by 20–25g of rhubarb compote before baking. After baking, spray the buns generously with vanilla syrup.

MILK SLICES

Makes 20 pieces

Chocolate sponge cake
150g white flour, 11% protein
200g salted butter
200g white sugar
230g eggs
4g baking powder
50g cocoa powder

Dulce de leche
1 can sweetened condensed milk

Italian meringue
225g egg whites
30g egg white powder
200g water
410g white sugar

Milk slice filling
900g mascarpone
200g white chocolate, melted

10g flakey sea salt, for garnish

Chocolate sponge cake
Preheat the oven to 180°C / 356°F on top and bottom heat setting. Line a 47 × 38cm / 18.5 × 15in baking tray with baking paper.

Scale all the ingredients and sieve the flour. In the bowl of a stand mixer with paddle attachment, mix butter and sugar together until combined, add the eggs gradually (one by one). Add the flour, baking powder and cocoa powder. Mix until combined.

Use a tiny amount of the cake mix to adhere the baking paper to your baking tray by adding a small bit under each corner of the paper. This will prevent the paper from shifting.

Transfer the cake batter to the lined baking tray. Using a pastry scraper and offset palette knife, spread 700g of the batter evenly on the tray. Transfer the tray to the middle rack of the oven and bake for about 7 minutes.

Remove the tray from the oven and allow the sponge to cool. Once cooled, cut the sponge in half, place it in a large plastic bag and store in the freezer until ready to assemble the cake. The cake sponge can also be left covered at room temperature; however, it is easier to work with from the freezer.

Dulce de leche
Place the can of condensed milk into a pan with water, bring it to boil and boil for 4.5 hours, adding water as needed. The can must always be submerged. Leave the tin to cool, without opening.

Italian meringue
Place the egg whites and egg white powder in the bowl of a stand mixer with the whisk attachment. Begin whisking at slow speed.

Scale the water and sugar into a pan with a heavy base on medium heat until the sugar reaches 115°C / 239°F. As soon as the temperature is reached, turn the stand mixer to high speed and whisk until soft peaks are formed. Bring the sugar temperature up to 121°C / 250°F, lower the mixing speed to medium and begin pouring a thin ribbon of syrup along the side of the mixing bowl into the egg whites. Once the sugar syrup is combined, increase the speed to high and mix for about 12 minutes, until it is cool, forming stiff peaks.

→

Filling
Place the mascarpone into a large mixing bowl.

Heat the white chocolate in a microwave or over a bain-marie (see page 336) until completely melted and quite hot. Place the hot white chocolate into a large mixing bowl.

Scale 500g of the Italian meringue. Place ¼ of the meringue into the white chocolate and whisk vigorously until combined. Add this mixture to the mascarpone and fold through until combined. Finally fold through the remainder of the meringue, creating a smooth and homogeneous filling.

Assembly
Remove the sponge from the freezer and place a piece topside down onto a papered tray (smooth side down). Add all the filling on top of the sponge and smooth out with a palette knife until even. Place the other sponge on top, topside up, and press lightly. Place the milk slice into the freezer and freeze for at least 4 hours, best overnight.

Serving
Open the can of condensed milk and transfer the dulce de leche to a piping bag. Remove the milk slice from the freezer and use a large chef's knife to cut it into 8 × 4cm / 3 × 1.5in rectangles. For cleaner cuts, the knife can be heated with a blowtorch or kept in warm water while cutting the cake.

Arrange each milk slice on a presentation tray and pipe waves of dulce de leche all the way along one side of the chocolate sponge. Garnish with a few flakes of sea salt.

OTHELLO CAKES

Makes 8 pieces

Diplomat cream (page 328)
200g diplomat cream
(requires 100g crème pâtissière)

Vanilla syrup (page 320)
50g, for dipping

Sponge
60g white sugar
100g egg yolks
60g corn starch
60g white flour, 11% protein
175g egg whites
60g white sugar

Dacquoise
125g extra fine almond flour
60g white flour, 11% protein
200g white sugar
250g egg whites
100g white sugar
8g egg white powder

Raspberry puree
200g raspberry puree
60g white sugar

Marzipan coating
400g white marzipan, 25% almond, 75% sugar, for decoration
Icing sugar, for rolling out

Bavaroise cream
105g milk, 3.5% fat
60g egg yolks
50g white sugar
3g gelatine (1 sheet)
200g cream, 38% fat

Chocolate ganache
50g dark chocolate, 60% cocoa
100g cream
12g glucose

Day 1

Crème pâtissière (page 326).
Prepare a batch and reserve it in the fridge until mixing the diplomat cream the following day.

Vanilla syrup (page 320)
Prepare the syrup and allow it to infuse till the following day.

Preheat the oven to 180°C / 356°F on the top and bottom heat setting. Spray a silicone Silpat baking mat with 1cm / 0.4in raised edges, 43cm by 36cm / 17 × 14.2in with fat using a spray bottle. Place the mat onto a large, heavy baking tray. It's important that the mat stays completely flat while baking.

Sponge
Set up a bain-marie (see page 336).

Scale sugar and egg yolks into the mixing bowl and whisk until the mixture reaches 40°C / 104°F. Transfer the mixture to the bowl of a stand mixer and, using the whisk attachment, mix on high speed until ribbons form. Transfer this mixture to a mixing bowl. Clean the bowl of the stand mixer.

Meringue
Place the egg whites into the bowl of the stand mixer and mix on medium speed for about 8–10 minutes, until soft peaks form. Begin adding the sugar, a small amount at a time. Adjust the speed of the mixer to low when adding sugar and then back up to medium to incorporate it. When all the sugar is added, the mixer should be on medium-high speed. Mix until stiff peaks form and the mixture is shiny and thick. Turn off the mixer.

Sponge (continued)
Sieve the flour and cornstarch for the sponge together into a bowl. In a large mixing bowl, fold the egg yolk mix and the meringue together. Then gently fold in the flour and corn starch, ensuring to keep as much air in the mixture as possible. Transfer the mixture into the sprayed Silpat mat. Use a palette knife to spread the batter until it is even and flat.

Place the baking tray into the oven on the middle rack and bake the sponge for 8 minutes. The cake should be ready when the edges pull away from the sides of the silicone mat. It is important not to over-bake and dry out the cake.

Take the cake out of the oven and allow it to cool completely before removing it from the silicone mat. Clean and re-spray the Silpat mat with the fat spray. It will be used again for the dacquoise.

→

Dacquoise
Preheat the oven to 180°C / 356°F on the top and bottom heat setting. Sift the flour into a bowl with the almond flour and sugar. Whisk to combine. Make the French meringue following the same process as above, except add the egg white powder to the egg whites at the beginning of mixing. The egg white powder creates a more stable meringue for the dacquoise batter.

Fold the meringue into the almond flour mixture until combined. Transfer the mixture onto the sprayed Silpat mat. Place the baking tray into the oven on the middle rack. Bake for about 13 minutes. Remove the cake from the oven and let it cool completely.

Cut out
Using a 6cm / 2.4in ring cutter, punch out the whole sheet of the sponge cake from above and the dacquoise. Place both sets of cake discs onto a tray with baking paper, wrap in cling film and store at room temperature until assembling the cake.

Raspberry puree
Place raspberry puree into a heavy bottomed pot and melt the puree slightly. Once there is a layer of liquid on the bottom of the pan, add in the sugar. Bring to boil and reduce for 2–3 minutes while stirring occasionally. Remove the pot from the heat and allow the puree to cool. When the puree is completely cool, transfer it to a piping bag.

Day 2

Marzipan coating
Lightly dust the work surface with icing sugar. Using a large rolling pin, roll out the marzipan block to 22cm long, about 10cm wide and 2mm thick / 8.7 × 4 × 0.08in.

Using a large chef's knife, cut 20cm / 8in strips lengthways, then using a fluted pasta wheel, cut each strip in half. This should provide 8 strips. If there are any issues, the marzipan can be kneaded back together and re-rolled. The final dimensions of each strip should be 5cm wide (top edge fluted), 20cm long, 2mm thick / 2 × 8 × 0.08in (it should be 5cm / 2in in height including the fluted edge). Place the marzipan strips on a tray with baking paper, tightly cover in plastic and store till assembly.

Diplomat cream
Use the crème pâtissière that was prepared the day before and make 200g of diplomat cream (page 328). Place the diplomat into a piping bag with a 13mm / 0.5in metal round nozzle.

→

Bavaroise cream
Place the milk in a large pot, bring it to boil and lower the heat. While the milk is heating, mix the yolks and sugar in a large mixing bowl. Slowly add the heated milk to the yolks and sugar. Transfer the mixture back to the pot and heat while stirring gently until it reaches 82°C / 180°F. Remove the pot from the heat.

With a large metal sieve, strain the mixture into a clean mixing bowl. Add the gelatine into the mixture. Cover the surface with cling film to prevent skin from forming. Put the pot in the fridge and chill until the mixture is 35°C / 95°F.

While the mixture is cooling, whip the cream until soft peaks form. Fold the whipped cream into the cooled custard mixture. Transfer the cream to a piping bag.

Assembly
Lay out the 8 metal rings, each 6cm / 2.4in diameter 5cm / 2in high, on a baking tray lined with baking paper. Prepare 8 strips of acetate, 20cm long and 6cm wide / 8 × 2.4in. Line the inside of the rings with acetate plastic.

The following can be done step by step for each of the 8 cakes: Start by dipping the discs of the sponge cake into the vanilla syrup for just a few seconds and set them aside on a tray lined with baking paper. Place 1 disc of the punched-out dacquoise into the base of the ring. Then pipe 6g of raspberry puree in an even layer into each ring. Pipe 18–20g of the bavaroise on top. Add 1 disc of the vanilla-soaked sponge. Add a second layer of 18–20g bavaroise.

Place the cakes in the freezer until they are completely frozen, about 2–3 hours. While the cakes are cooling down, prepare the ganache.

Chocolate ganache
Chop the chocolate into small pieces and place them in a heat-proof mixing bowl. Heat the cream and glucose in a saucepan until steaming. Pour the cream onto the chocolate. Gently mix with a silicone spatula to cover the chocolate in the hot cream and then allow the mixture to stand for 1 minute.

Using an immersion blender (or just the silicone spatula from before), mix together until the ganache is thick, glossy and fully incorporated. Allow the ganache to cool slightly and transfer it to a small jug with a pouring spout.

→

Final assembly

Remove the cakes from the freezer. Add 15g ganache on top of each, lifting and rotating each to create an even layer. Put the cakes back in the freezer until the ganache is set.

Carefully push the cakes up from the bottom to remove them from the ring. Peel away the acetate. Leave the cakes to defrost to room temperature.

Once defrosted, wrap the marzipan around each Othello cake with the fluted side up. Pipe 20g of the diplomat cream into one corner of the Othello, leaving a small gap of ganache still exposed. Using a teaspoon dipped in warm water, create a small dimple on top of the diplomat. Pipe in a small amount of the raspberry puree.

©2022

SUMMER

STRAWBERRY CREAM BUNS
STRAWBERRY BRIOCHE
MARGRETHE CAKES
RASPBERRY TARTS
BLACKBERRY AND HAZELNUT FRANGIPANE TARTS
BLACKCURRANT CREAM BUNS

The summer may be short in Denmark, but when it arrives it transforms Copenhagen into a place humming with life and joy. The days are long, and people are eager to savour the fleeting season that is wrapped in an abundance of flavours. For just a few weeks the bakery overflows with fruits and berries so ripe they seem almost otherworldly, packed with sweetness and goodness. Strawberries always arrive first, then the raspberries, followed by blackberries and more. Our most beloved summer pastries each consist of simple ingredients coming together in perfect harmony. Summer at the bakery is about letting the soft, juicy fruits and berries shine, paired with the lightest doughs or a cloud of whipped vanilla custard, sometimes resting gently in a crisp sablé tart. It is a celebration of simplicity, freshness and the pure joy of tasting Danish summer at its peak.

STRAWBERRY CREAM BUNS

Makes 8 buns

Buns
8 baked cream buns (page 140)

Filling
450g diplomat cream (page 328)
250g strawberries

Garnish
30g salted butter
200g white sugar
5 large strawberries, sliced vertically

Buns
Roll, prove and bake 8 cream buns (see page 140). Prepare the crème pâtissière for the diplomat cream and cool it down.

While the cream buns are cooling down, mix 450g of diplomat cream (page 328).

Filling and garnishing
Chop the strawberries finely and drain the excess juice through a metal sieve. Transfer the chopped strawberries to a piping bag.

Use a sharp knife to poke a small hole in the base of each bun. Insert the tip of the piping bag with the chopped strawberries and pipe about 25g into each bun.

Using another piping bag, insert a 13mm / 0.5in nozzle and fill the bag with the diplomat cream. Pipe about 35–40g of diplomat cream into each bun. Use a pastry scraper to remove any excess filling afterwards.

Melt the butter and evenly brush each bun. Allow the butter to set for a few minutes.

Transfer each bun into a bowl with the sugar and coat them completely. Move the buns to a presentation tray and pipe a small spire of diplomat cream on top. Garnish with 1 slice of strawberry with the tip pointing up.

STRAWBERRY BRIOCHE

Makes 12 pieces

Brioche (page 120)
1 block of laminated brioche dough

Diplomat cream (page 328)
360g

Strawberry compote
150g strawberries
50g white sugar

Rhubarb compote
100g rhubarb
50g white sugar

Topping
200g strawberries, chopped
6g strawberry compote
Zest of half a lemon

Sugar crust
200g raw cane sugar
50g salted butter, melted

Prepare crème pâtissière for the diplomat cream, make the compotes and divide the laminated brioche dough.

Strawberry compote
Place both the strawberries and the sugar into a saucepan. On a medium low heat, stir the mixture regularly in the beginning to prevent it sticking to the bottom. Once the mass is mostly liquid, you can leave it to boil, stirring occasionally. Using a thermometer, check the temperature of the jam. When it reaches between 98 and 100°C / 208–212°F, remove it from the heat. Place the jam into a bowl and cover the surface with cling film to prevent skin from forming.

Rhubarb compote
Follow the same procedure as shown on page 204 (rhubarb buns). This compote only needs to be cooked until there are no lumps of rhubarb left so a temperature does not need to be taken.

Compote mixture
In a bowl, measure the weight of the entire mass of rhubarb compote. It should be roughly 100g. Mix in an equal amount of the strawberry compote so it is a 1:1 ratio. The remaining strawberry compote will be used for the topping.

Dough
Remove the rested laminated brioche dough from the fridge and begin rolling it out to 4.5mm thick, 18cm high and 36cm long / 0.18 × 7 × 14in. Measure the rectangle into 9 by 9cm / 3.5 × 3.5in squares. Divide using a sharp knife. Place the squares onto a tray lined with baking paper, wrap it tightly in cling film and store in the fridge overnight or at least until completely firm so that it can be coated in sugar without distorting the shape.

Line a baking tray with baking paper. Put the raw cane sugar for the sugar coating into a wide container. Remove the brioches from the fridge. Brush each piece with melted butter. Place it into the raw cane sugar and coat both sides, then transfer to the baking tray leaving 3–4cm / 1.2–1.5in between each piece.

Place the tray in a warm humid place and prove at 28°C / 82°F for about 1.5 hours (see proving advice, page 32).

After 1 hour, preheat the oven to 190°C / 374°F on convection setting.

→

When ready to bake, the squares should have expanded by about 35% and the layers should start to separate. At the bakery, we slightly under-prove the dough at this stage to ensure the beautiful layers are as defined as possible.

Take a corner of one piece, stretch outward, then fold the corner back toward the centre. Repeat with the other corners, folding in each to meet in the centre. Press down gently on top of where the 4 meet in the middle. On top of this, spoon on about 15g of strawberry and rhubarb mixture.

Place the tray into the oven on the middle rack and bake for 8 minutes. Turn the tray to ensure even baking and bake for another 4–5 minutes, until the edges of the brioches are golden brown.

Allow them to cool completely.

Finishing
Prepare the diplomat cream and transfer it into a piping bag with a 13mm / 0.5in round metal nozzle. In the centre of each brioche, pipe a low dome of diplomat cream, about 30g. Take a spoon and dip it into warm water. Using gentle pressure, make an indent in the diplomat cream that is large enough to hold the strawberry topping.

Finally, take a spoonful of the strawberry topping mixture and carefully place it in the centre. Make sure to get some of the syrup from the bottom of the bowl for an extra beautiful finish on the top.

MARGRETHE CAKES

Makes 8 cakes

Strawberry puree
250g strawberry puree
100g white sugar

Elderflower jelly
200g elderflower cordial
3g gelatine leaf, soaked in cold water

Strawberries
250g fresh ripe strawberries
10g elderflowers for garnish

The Margrethe cake is our seasonal variation of the Othello cake (page 210). Follow the same procedure, except that diplomat cream and chocolate ganache are not required, and that raspberry puree for the Othello is replaced by strawberry puree. The cakes are finished with a layer of sliced fresh strawberries coated in elderflower jelly.

Day 1
Prepare the crème pâtissière, bavarois cream, cake bases and vanilla syrup as for the Othello cake, and strawberry puree and elderflower jelly.

Strawberry puree
Place the ingredients in a pan, bring it to boil and reduce for 2–3 minutes. Leave the puree to cool and transfer it to a piping bag. Store in the fridge.

Elderflower jelly
Warm half of the cordial in a pot on medium heat and add gelatine to dissolve, add the remaining cordial and stir to combine. Cool and reserve the jelly.

Day 2
Follow the same steps as for the Othello cakes, prepare the marzipan sheets, metal rings and acetate strips.

Strawberries
Destem and slice the strawberries into quarters.

Assembly
Set up 8 metal rings, 6cm diameter and 5cm high / 2.4 × 2in on a baking tray lined with baking paper, and place a strip of acetate on the inside of each ring.

Start by dipping the discs of the sponge cake into the vanilla syrup for just a few seconds and set them aside on a tray lined with baking paper.

The steps below can be done step by step for each of the 8 cakes:

Place 1 disc of the punched out dacquoise into the base of a ring. Pipe 35–40g of the bavarois on top. Place 15g of sliced strawberries into the bavarois and spread them evenly. Add 1 disc of the sponge that was soaked in vanilla syrup. Pipe 10g strawberry puree in an even layer.

Put the cakes in the freezer to set for 2–3 hours until completely frozen.

→

Final assembly
Slice the remaining strawberries into 5mm / 0.2in thick rounds.

Remove the cakes from the freezer, make sure they are completely set. If not, return to the freezer and check every 30 minutes. Carefully remove the cakes from the rings and peel away the acetate. Once defrosted, wrap the marzipan around each cake with the fluted side up. Lay the strawberry slices on top, following the shape of the ring and overlapping the edges in the shape of a rose. Return the cakes to the freezer.

Warm up the elderflower jelly till a liquid consistency. Add a layer of elderflower jelly on top of the cakes to cover the strawberries. Place the cakes in the freezer to set for 20 minutes.

Leave the cakes to defrost slightly if serving immediately or store them in the fridge. Finish with a few elderflower blossoms.

RASPBERRY TARTS

Makes 10 tarts

Mazarine
100g salted butter
125g marzipan, 66% almond, 34% sugar, soft
100g white sugar
100g eggs
125g white flour, 11% protein
7g salt

Sablé for 10 tarts (page 332)

Mascarpone cream
75g mascarpone
20g white sugar
25g cream, 38% fat
¼ of a vanilla pod, scraped

Raspberry topping
300g ripe raspberries

Rose syrup (page 324)
50g

Sablé
Prepare the sablé and line ten 10cm / 8in tart tins with it. Reserve them in the fridge until all the other elements are ready.

Mazarine
To prepare the mazarine, start with the brown butter.

Brown butter
Melt the butter in a medium-sized frying pan or skillet over medium heat. A light-coloured pan is best so that you can monitor the browning process. Swirl the pan occasionally to make sure the butter is cooking evenly. Once the butter turns a nutty brown, take it off the heat and transfer to a heat-proof bowl. Place in the fridge and store until the butter is set to a similar consistency to regular cold butter, about 1 hour, depending on your fridge temperature.

Preheat the oven to 190°C / 374°F on the top and bottom heat setting.

Mixing
Place the marzipan and sugar in the food processor and pulse until combined. While the food processor is still running, start adding the brown butter relatively quickly so not to split the marzipan.

Once the butter is incorporated, turn off the food processor. Transfer the mixture to the bowl of a stand mixer with a paddle attachment and incrementally add the eggs, salt and flour until combined. Once the mazarine is homogeneous, scrape down the bowl to make sure all the ingredients are well incorporated and mix again for a minute till combined.

Transfer into a piping bag.

Piping and baking
Pipe about 25g of mazarine into each tart. Transfer the tarts to a heavy baking tray and place it in the oven on the middle rack. Bake for about 13 minutes at 190°C / 374°F, carefully turning the tray halfway through to ensure even baking.

Remove the tray from the oven and leave the tarts to cool slightly before removing them from the tins.

→

Mascarpone cream
Place the mascarpone, cream, sugar and vanilla into the bowl of a stand mixer. Using the whisk attachment, whip the mixture into medium peaks (if unsure about the texture you can drop a quenelle onto a plate, the quenelle should hold its shape). Finish mixing the cream and reserve it in the fridge until needed.

Raspberry topping
Finely chop about 150g of the raspberries, carefully draining off the excess juice. Cut the rest of the raspberries in halves lengthwise, stem to point.

Assembly
Spread an even layer of chopped raspberries on top of the mazarine tarts. Arrange the sliced raspberries around the edge of the tarts, making sure they are an even distance apart from each other, creating a rose shape. Spray the tarts with a light mist of rose syrup for flavour and shine.

Lastly, quenelle the mascarpone cream and place the quenelles in the centre of the tarts.

BLACKBERRY AND HAZELNUT FRANGIPANE TARTS

Makes 10 tarts

Sablé for 10 tarts (page 332)
350g hazelnut frangipane in piping bag (page 334)
350g blackberries
Icing sugar for dusting, if needed

Frangipane and sablé
Prepare the classic sablé (page 332) and the hazelnut frangipane (page 334) and line ten 8cm / 3in tart tins, with the sablé.

Preheat the oven to 190°C / 374°F on top and bottom heat setting.

Piping
Pipe about 35g of hazelnut frangipane into each tart. Leave the tarts at room temperature.

Finishing
Gently press 4–5 pieces into each tart. The size of blackberries varies greatly, so if they are very large, slice them in half, and adjust as needed to the fruit of the season.

Baking
Transfer the tarts to a heavy baking tray and place it on the centre rack of the oven. Bake for about 17 minutes, carefully turning the tray halfway through to ensure even baking.

Remove the tarts from the oven and leave them to cool slightly before turning them out of the tins.

When cool dust the tarts lightly with icing sugar.

BLACKCURRANT CREAM BUNS

Makes 8 buns

Buns
8 baked cream buns (page 140)

Garnish
30g salted butter
30g whole blackcurrants
30g white sugar

Filling
400g diplomat cream (page 328)
175g blackcurrant puree
45g white sugar

Buns
Roll, prove and bake 8 cream buns (see page 140). Prepare the crème pâtissière for the diplomat cream and cool it down.

While the cream buns are cooling down, mix 400g of diplomat cream (page 328).

Garnish
Toss the whole blackcurrants with sugar and leave in the fridge to macerate.

Filling
Place the puree and sugar in a saucepan and, while whisking continuously, bring it to 101°C / 214°F. Allow the mixture to cool completely and transfer it to a piping bag.

Use a sharp knife to poke a small hole in the base of each bun. Insert the tip of the piping bag with the blackcurrant puree and pipe about 20–25g into each bun.

Using another piping bag, insert a 13mm / 0.5in nozzle and fill the bag with the diplomat cream. Pipe about 35–40g of diplomat cream into each bun. Use a pastry scraper to remove any excess filling.

Melt the butter and evenly brush each bun. Allow the butter to set for a few minutes.

Transfer each bun to a bowl with the sugar and coat them completely. Move the buns to a presentation tray and pipe a small spire of diplomat cream on top. Garnish with 1 black-currant berry on top of each spire.

RALEIGH

AUTUMN

TARTE TATIN
APPLE AND HAZELNUT FRANGIPANE TARTS
APPLE CRUMBLE BRIOCHE
HAZELNUT CREAM PUFFS
HAZELNUT AND POPPYSEED COOKIES
PEAR AND PISTACHIO FRANGIPANE TARTS
DREAM CAKE

As temperatures drop and the days become shorter, a certain mood begins to settle in. The warm cup of coffee suddenly brings extra comfort, and the scents of baked apples, toasted nuts and warm spices infuse the bakery with a comforting fragrance. This is what autumn is all about – comfort. Or as we say in Denmark: hygge. There are hundreds of apple varieties in Denmark, some sweet and firm, others more perfumed and brittle. We are lucky to work with Anders and Susanne, who from their orchard supply us through the season with Danish heirloom varieties of both apples and pears. 'Discovery' is an early apple variety that, with its beautiful bright red colour and wonderful aroma, has become a favourite, especially for the tarte tatin!

TARTE TATIN

Makes one tart

Puff pastry
375g white flour, 12% protein
7g salt
185g water

Lamination butter
300g salted butter

Apples
7–8 apples

Caramel sauce
70g cream, 38% fat
70g white sugar

For base of mould
125g salted butter
125g white sugar

Mascarpone cream (page 234)
100g

Day 1
Scale all of the ingredients for the puff pastry. In the bowl of a stand mixer with the hook attachment, mix the water, flour and salt for about 5 minutes at slow speed. Scrape down the sides and mix again for about 2 minutes at second speed.

Remove the dough from the mixer and shape into a ball. Cut a deep X in the surface with a sharp knife. Press the corners to form a square. Wrap the dough tightly in a plastic bag or in plastic wrap and reserve in the fridge until the next day.

Day 2
Using baking paper, prepare a 300g butter sheet, the same size as the dough, and about 2cm / 0.8in thick. If the butter becomes too warm, let it cool down in the fridge until beginning lamination (see lamination guide, page 88). Making puff pastry requires 5 single folds, resting 30 minutes between each fold.

After the final fold, let the dough rest overnight in the fridge.

Day 3
Roll the dough down to 3.5mm / 0.14in thick and allow it to rest for 4 hours in the fridge. Then cut the puff pastry into a 25cm / 10in diameter circle. This will be the sheet for the top of the tarte tatin. Store in the fridge until use.

Preheat the oven to 190°C / 374°F on top and bottom heat setting. Cut out a disc of baking paper to the exact size of the baking tin and place it in the bottom of this.

Take the 125g butter and roll it out between baking papers, until round and roughly the size of the base of the baking tin. Remove the top layer of baking paper and place the butter disc in the bottom of the baking tin, with the exposed side up, baking paper side down. Sprinkle 125g sugar in an even layer on top of the butter disc.

Apples
Peel the apples, remove the cores and cut them into quarters. Using a turning knife, trim the edges of the apple quarters to achieve smooth edges.

Mascarpone cream
Prepare the mascarpone cream (see page 234) and store in the fridge until serving.

→

Assembly
Place an apple quarter in the centre of the baking tin, core-side up, and another on top, core-side down.

Arrange the rest of the apple quarters in a spiral around the centre apples, leaving a small gap between them so the apples can slip into place when baking. Place the puff pastry sheet on top of the apples and gently tuck in the edges.

Transfer the baking tin to the middle rack of the oven and bake the tarte for 1 hour 40 minutes.

Remove the tray from the oven and allow the tarte to cool for about 15 minutes. Prepare another baking tray with baking paper, place the tray with the paper on top of the tarte tatin and in one motion flip everything to transfer the tarte to the tray apple-side up.

Caramel sauce
Warm the cream on low heat in a pot. Reserve on low heat.

In a heavy based pot, add one third of the sugar and melt on medium heat until the sugar is dissolved. Add the next third of sugar and let it dissolve. Repeat with the final third, stirring gently. Once the sugar starts to caramelise and begins to bubble in the centre, stop stirring. When the colour is a rich golden brown, turn off the heat. Stir the heated cream into the caramel with the heat off.

Finishing
Generously spoon the caramel sauce over the top of the apples. Allow the tarte tatin to cool completely. Serve with quenelles of the mascarpone cream.

APPLE AND HAZELNUT FRANGIPANE TARTS

Makes 10 tarts

Sablé for 10 tarts (page 332)
350g hazelnut frangipane in piping bag (page 334)
6–8 medium apples
20g raw cane sugar

Frangipane and sablé
Prepare the classic sablé (page 332) and the hazelnut frangipane (page 334) and line ten 8cm / 3in tart tins with the sablé.

Piping
Pipe about 35g of hazelnut frangipane into each tart. Leave the tarts at room temperature while preparing the apples. If it takes longer than 15 minutes to mandolin the apples, or if the room is warm, place the tarts in the fridge. Just make sure to take them out again to room temperature about 10 minutes before adding the apples.

Preheat the oven to 190°C / 374°F on top and bottom heat setting.

Apple slicing
Use a Japanese spiralizer mandolin. Place the green piece on one side of the metal piece, insert the metal piece directly through the centre of the apple, then add the last green piece into the apple on the other side. Attach the metal bar into the mandolin, move the slide lever down and move the blade near to the apple while rotating the handle. Apply as much pressure as is required to create a consistent slice 1mm / 0.04in thick and the width of the apple.

After slicing, take the strip of apple, lay it onto the tabletop and cut it in half across the width. Carefully roll the apple slices into a rose shape. Depending on the size of the apple, add 2–3 strips of apple together, wrapping each piece around the roll creating a rose. Make 10 roses in total.

Finishing
One by one, place each rose on top of the soft frangipane and lightly sprinkle raw cane sugar onto the apple. Avoid sugar falling on the edge of the tart as this may cause it to stick.

Baking
Transfer the tarts to a heavy baking tray and place it on the centre rack of the oven. Bake for about 17 minutes, carefully turning the tray halfway through to ensure even baking.

Remove the tarts from the oven and leave them to cool slightly before turning them out of the tins.

かつらむき
つまきり
あみきり
つま太郎
1台3役
CHIBA
MADE IN JAPAN

APPLE CRUMBLE BRIOCHE

Makes 12 pieces

Brioche (page 120)
1 block of laminated brioche dough

Apple compote
300g apples
30g salted butter, soft
30g white sugar

Crumble topping
50g white flour
50g raw cane sugar
1g vanilla sugar
1g ground cinnamon
35g salted butter, cold

Sugar crust
50g salted butter, melted
200g raw cane sugar

Prepare the apple compote and the crumble and divide the laminated brioche dough.

Apple compote
Preheat the oven to 250°C / 482°F on top and bottom heat setting. Line a heavy baking tray with baking paper.

Core and roughly chop the apples into large chunks. In a large bowl, coat the apples with soft butter and sugar. Transfer to the baking tray and spread in an even layer.

Bake for about 25 minutes, then check, add time in 5-minute intervals until the apples are lightly caramelised and completely soft. Remove them from the oven and let them cool for a few minutes. While they are still warm, carefully transfer the apples to a steel bowl and gently mix the compote together with a whisk, until a rough texture is achieved. Allow it to cool and store in the fridge overnight.

Crumble topping
Scale the flour, sugar, vanilla sugar and cinnamon together in a mixing bowl. Chop the butter in small cubes. Using your fingers, crumble together the butter into the flour mixture until it becomes a rough sandy texture with big and small pieces. It is important not to over-mix the crumble. Store overnight in the fridge.

Dough
Remove the rested laminated brioche dough from the fridge and begin rolling it out to 4.5mm thick, 18cm high and 36cm long / 0.18 × 7 × 14in. Measure the rectangle into 9 by 9cm / 3.5 × 3.5in squares. Divide using a sharp knife. Place the squares onto a tray lined with baking paper, wrap it tightly in cling film and store in the fridge overnight or at least until completely firm so that it can be coated in sugar without distorting the shape.

Proving
Line a baking tray with baking paper. Put the raw cane sugar for the sugar coating into a wide container. Remove the brioches from the fridge. Brush each piece with melted butter. Place it into the raw cane sugar and coat both sides, then transfer to the baking tray leaving 3–4cm / 1.2–1.5in between each piece.

Put the tray in a warm, humid place and prove at 28°C / 82°F for about 1.5 hours (see proving advice, page 32).

After 1 hour, preheat the oven to 190°C / 374°F on convection setting.

→

When ready to bake, the squares should have expanded by about 35% and the layers should start to separate. In the bakery, we slightly under-prove the dough at this stage to ensure the beautiful layers are as defined as possible.

Take one corner of a piece, stretch outward, then fold the corner back toward the centre. Repeat with the other corners, folding in each to meet in the centre. Press down gently on top of where the four meet in the middle. On top of this, spoon on about 30g of apple compote and dress with about 15g of rough chunks of crumble.

Baking
Place the tray into the oven on the middle rack and bake for 8 minutes. Turn the tray to ensure even baking and bake for another 4–5 minutes, until the edges of the brioches are golden brown.

Allow them to cool completely.

HAZELNUT CREAM PUFFS

Makes 12 pieces

Crème pâtissière (page 326)
500g

Craquelin
60g salted butter, soft
80g white sugar
80g white flour, 11% protein

Choux
45g milk, 3.5% fat
45g water
40g salted butter
60g white flour, 11% protein, sieved
95g eggs, beaten
1g salt

Ganache montée
40g milk chocolate, 50% cocoa
40g cream, 38% fat
5g glucose
5g honey
½ gelatine leaf, soaked in cold water
45g cold cream, 38% fat
125g crème pâtissière (page 326)

Praline cream
100g salted butter, soft
375g crème pâtissière (page 326)
240g praline paste, 50% hazelnut, 50% sugar
150g cream, 38% fat

Caramelised hazelnuts, for hazelnut praline and garnishing
150g hazelnuts, peeled, roasted
125g white sugar

Hazelnut praline
75g (from the above caramelised hazelnuts)
Pinch of sea salt

Feuilletine discs
190g Gianduja, 35% hazelnut
75g feuilletine flakes

Prepare all the elements the day before serving. On the following day, bake the choux and assemble the elements.

Day 1

Crème pâtissière (page 326)
Start by making the crème pâtissière so that it has time to set for at least 2–3 hours in the fridge before preparing the other creams. It will be used both in the ganache montèe and the praline cream.

Craquelin
Mix everything together in the bowl of a stand mixer with a paddle attachment just until combined. Transfer the dough to the table and finish combining by hand. Roll the mixture out between two pieces of baking paper to 2mm / 0.08in thick. Chill in the freezer for about 1 hour.

Remove the craquelin from the freezer, allow it to warm up slightly then punch out discs with a 6cm / 2.4in diameter cutter. Store the discs in the fridge.

Choux
Line a baking tray which should be able to fit into the freezer with baking paper.

Place milk, water and butter into a saucepan and bring to a boil. Remove the pot from the heat, add the sieved flour and stir vigorously until well combined. Place the pot back onto medium heat and begin to cook out for about 5 minutes. The aim here is to evaporate some of the moisture from the roux. A good test of when the roux is cooked out enough is when a film forms on the bottom of the pan.

Transfer the mixture into the bowl of a stand mixer with the paddle attachment. Mix for 3–4 minutes until the mix slightly cools.

In a separate bowl, whisk the eggs together with salt. While continuing to mix, gradually add the eggs to the roux a little bit at a time, making sure the egg is fully incorporated before adding more. The choux paste should become smooth and slightly glossy.

The amount of egg needed may vary depending on how much moisture you cooked out of your roux. As a result of this, the best way to know if the choux (paste) is ready is to dip the paddle attachment into the centre of the mixture and pull up. The paste should slowly drop, leaving a 'V' shape of paste on the paddle.

Transfer the choux to a piping bag with a 13mm / 0.5in round nozzle.

→

Piping
Pipe the choux in 12 even rounds of 16–18g onto a baking tray lined with baking paper. Leave about 3–4cm / 1.2–1.5in between each.

Once piped, place the round discs of craquelin on top of the choux, making sure it is placed in the centre. Transfer the tray to the freezer.

Ganache montée
Chop the chocolate into small pieces and place them in a heat-proof mixing bowl. Heat the cream, glucose and honey in a saucepan until steaming. Pour the cream over the chocolate and let it melt the chocolate for 1–2 minutes. Gently mix with a spatula. Add the gelatine and mix gently. Finally add the cold cream and mix until the ganache is homogeneous.

Pass it through a metal sieve and place it in an airtight container, with a layer of cling film on the surface to prevent skin from forming. Store the ganache in the fridge overnight.

Praline cream
Gently warm the butter in the microwave until it is soft. Place the crème pâtissière and the praline paste in the bowl of a stand mixer with a whisk attachment. Whisk on medium speed until combined. Scrape down the sides of the bowl to get rid of any remaining praline. Continue mixing on medium speed, add the soft butter and mix until incorporated. It is very important not to over-mix. Transfer the praline cream to another bowl.

In the stand mixer, whip the fresh cream to medium-soft peaks. Using a spatula, fold the cream one third at a time into the praline mixture until fully incorporated. Transfer the cream to an airtight container and set in the fridge overnight.

Place it into a piping bag with a 10mm / 0.4in star nozzle.

Caramelised hazelnuts
Warm up the hazelnuts in the microwave.

In a heavy-based pot on medium heat, add one third of the sugar. When the sugar melts, repeat with the remaining two thirds. Raise the temperature to about 160°C / 320°F. You are looking for sugar granules to be dissolved and for the caramel to have a rich golden colour. Turn off the heat. Add the hazelnuts to the caramel and stir to coat them completely. Remove from the pan and transfer to a tray with baking paper, separating the hazelnuts while they are hot. Allow them to cool.

→

Hazelnut praline
Put 75g of the hazelnuts and a pinch of sea salt in a food processor and blitz till a smooth praline. Place it into a piping bag.

Save the remaining hazelnuts for garnishing the choux.

Feuilletine discs
Chop the Gianduja into small pieces and melt it over a bain-marie (see page 336). Once melted, remove the Gianduja from the heat and add the feuilletine flakes. Allow the mixture to cool and move it onto a baking paper. Place another baking paper on top and roll until it is 2mm / 0.08in thick. Place it in the fridge to set for about 2 hours or until solid.

When it is set, punch the sheet out into twelve 6.5cm / 2.5in discs using a round cutter. Store the discs in the fridge.

Day 2
Preheat the oven to 180°C / 356°F on the convection setting.

Ganache montée
Remove the ganache from the fridge and transfer it to a large mixing bowl.

In a separate bowl, whisk 125g crème pâtissière until it is smooth, then fold the ganache and crème pâtissière together until combined. Transfer it to a piping bag and store it in the fridge.

Choux baking
Remove the tray of choux from the freezer and place it into the middle rack of the oven. Bake for 26 minutes until light golden brown. Allow the choux to cool completely.

Assembly
For each piece:
Slice off the top third of the choux. Pipe 18g of ganache montée into the base of the choux and add a pinch of sea salt. Place a feuilletine disc on top. Pipe about 60g of the praline cream in a swirling motion, raising the bag gradually while piping, keeping the same amount of pressure. Finally pipe 4g of the hazelnut praline into the centre of the praline cream. Place the lid of the choux on top. Garnish with 4–5 pieces of caramelised hazelnuts on the edges of the exposed praline cream.

HAZELNUT AND POPPYSEED COOKIES

Makes 40 cookies

135g salted butter
70g white sugar
50g brown sugar
160g white flour, 11% protein
50g whole-grain Einkorn flour, finely milled
4g baking powder
1g salt
15g milk, 3.5% fat
55g hazelnuts, chopped in halves

Coating
35g white poppyseeds
65g black poppyseeds

Mixing
Mix all the ingredients together, except for the hazelnuts and milk, until a crumbly consistency. Add the milk, followed by the hazelnuts. Split the dough in halves.

On a lightly floured work surface, knead the dough together slightly and carefully roll each half into an even log shape, 30cm / 12in long.

Preheat the oven to 165°C / 329°F on the convection setting. Line a baking tray with baking paper.

Coating and cutting
Mix the white and black poppyseeds and spread the mix on the table. Roll the logs of cookie dough into the poppyseed mix, ensuring the surface is completely coated. Put the logs in the fridge to chill and set for about 30 minutes to 1 hour, depending on the fridge temperature.

Cut the logs into about 20 rounds of 12g each. Arrange them on the baking tray lined with baking paper and place in the oven on the middle rack.

Bake the cookies for 14 minutes. Remove from the oven and allow them to cool.

PEAR AND PISTACHIO FRANGIPANE TARTS

Makes 10 tarts

Sablé for 10 tarts (page 332)
350g pistachio frangipane in piping bag (page 334)
4–5 small-medium pears, Conference or Clara Frijs

Anise poaching syrup
500g water
500g white sugar
5g green anise seed
1 lemon, peel

Frangipane and sablé
Prepare the classic sablé (page 332), the pistachio frangipane (page 334) and line ten 8cm / 3in tart tins with the sablé.

Anise poaching syrup
Place water and sugar in a pan and bring to the boil. Pour the boiling syrup over the anise seed and lemon peel and let it infuse for 20 minutes. Strain the syrup through a sieve and back into the pan, place it on the stove and bring the syrup to a simmer.

Pears
Leaving the skin on, slice the pears in half. Depending on the quality and texture of the pears that you use, it may be necessary to carefully remove any firm seeds from the centre of each half. With the Clara Frjis pears that we normally use, it is only at the very end of the season that the seeds are too firm.

Preheat the oven to 190°C / 374°F on the top and bottom heat setting.

Poaching
Transfer the pear halves into the poaching syrup. Poach in the syrup, turning them occasionally to ensure an even texture and continue poaching until you can easily pierce the pear with the tip of a knife. Remove each half from the syrup and place them on a tray to cool, allowing any excess syrup to drip away.

Sieve the remaining poaching liquid and leave it to chill. It can be placed in the fridge for further use / next time. Reserve a small amount of syrup to finish the tarts.

Finishing
While the poached pear halves are cooling down, pipe about 35g of pistachio frangipane into each tart shell. Place one pear half into the centre of the frangipane, pushing down slightly so it fixes into place.

Baking
Transfer the tarts to a heavy baking tray and place it on the centre rack of the oven. Bake the tarts for about 17 minutes, carefully turning the tray halfway through to ensure even baking.

Remove the tarts from the oven and leave them to cool slightly. While still warm, gently remove each tart from the tin and brush or mist the surface with the anise syrup you reserved.

DREAM CAKE

Makes one 500g cake

Batter
80g almond flour
145g white sugar
20g vanilla sugar
3g salt
90g salted butter
110g eggs
20g rum
100g white flour, 11% protein
3g baking powder

Tonka bean mix
2g tonka beans
18g coffee beans

Coconut topping
65g milk, 3.5% fat
85g salted butter
125g brown sugar
125g coconut flour
2g salt
4g tonka bean mix

Preheat the oven to 160°C / 320°F on the top and bottom heat setting. Grease a baking tin, 10cm deep, 10cm wide, 18cm long / 4 × 4 × 7in, cut baking paper to the size of the tin and line it with the paper.

Batter
Scale the ingredients and sift the flour. Put the almond flour, sugar, vanilla sugar and salt in the bowl of a stand mixer with the paddle attachment and mix until combined. Add the butter to the mixture one third at a time and mix at slow speed until combined. Scrape down the edges of the bowl using a pastry card.

Whisk together the eggs and rum. Then gradually begin adding the eggs and rum until combined. Scrape down the sides. Add the sifted flour and the baking powder. Mix until just combined. Gently transfer the batter to the lined baking tin.

Baking
Put the tin in the oven on the middle rack. Bake the cake for 42 minutes. While the cake is baking, prepare the topping.

Tonka bean mix
Blend tonka and coffee beans in a spice grinder.

Coconut topping
Put the milk and butter in a pot and warm the mixture on low heat until the butter is melted. Add brown sugar, coconut flour, salt and tonka and coffee bean mix. Remove the pot from the heat and mix well until the brown sugar is dissolved.

Finishing
Take the cake out of the oven. Allow it to cool slightly, then spread the coconut topping onto the cake and smooth it out until flat and even. Return the cake to the oven for 5 minutes. Allow the cake to cool completely before carefully removing it from the tin.

GRAM
LAMINATION FREEZER
GRAM
LAMINATION FRIDGE

CHRISTMAS

LUCIA BUNS
SAFFRON CAKE
PEPPARKAKOR
ORANGE CONFIT
FRENCH NOUGAT
ROCHER
MENDIANTS
KRANSEKAGE

The scent of saffron and its deep aroma means Christmas has arrived at the bakery. Together with the Lucia buns, the saffron buns are not only a seasonal highlight, but one of our most beloved pastries. In December, we also take the time to make all the little candies and chocolate we love ourselves. Confit orange peel, French nougat, rocher and more. Perfect additions to the Christmas celebrations. And so, the year comes to an end with the last piece of pastry, our kransekage that we scent with citrus zest and is traditionally eaten at midnight with a glass of champagne.

LUCIA BUNS

Makes 10 buns

850g saffron dough (page 142)
20g raisins for topping

Egg wash
2 whole eggs, beaten

Dough and shaping
Divide the saffron dough into 85g pieces. Pre-shape the pieces into 5cm / 2in oblong shapes. Let the dough rest for 10 minutes in the fridge.

Roll each piece into an even log shape, 35cm / 14in long, with slightly tapered ends. Rotate the left and the right sides of each piece towards the centre, forming two coils and creating an S-shape. Press a few raisins into the centre of both coils.

Let the buns prove in a humid place at 28–30°C / 82–86°F for 1–1.5 hours (see proving guide, page 32).

Baking
Preheat the oven to 200°C / 392°F using a convection setting. Egg wash the buns using a pastry brush before baking. Bake the buns for 7 minutes, turn the tray and bake another 2–3 minutes until the buns are light golden brown. It's important to bake as lightly as possible to retain moisture.

SAFFRON CAKE

Makes one 500g cake

Batter

Zest and juice from ¼ of an orange
85g white flour, 11% protein
100g almond flour
180g white sugar
2g salt
110g salted butter
135g eggs
10g saffron syrup (page 142)
4g baking powder

Citrus syrup

24g orange juice
2g lemon juice
20g white sugar
15g water

Day 1

Prepare the saffron syrup (page 142).

Day 2

Preheat your oven to 160°C / 320°F on the top and bottom heat setting. Grease a baking tin, 10cm deep, 10cm wide, 18cm long / 4 × 4 × 7in, and cut baking paper to the size of it.

Mixing

Juice the quarter of orange and zest the peel. Scale the ingredients and sift the flour. Put the almond flour, sugar and salt in the bowl of a stand mixer with paddle attachment and mix until combined. Add the butter to the mixture, one third at a time, and mix at slow speed until combined. Scrape down the edges of the bowl using a pastry card. Then add the saffron syrup and begin adding the eggs gradually until combined. Scrape down the sides. Add the flour and the baking powder. Mix until just combined. Gently transfer the batter into the lined cake tin.

Put the cake in the oven and bake for 45 minutes on the middle rack. Take it out and allow to cool for 20–30 minutes. While the cake is cooling down, prepare the citrus syrup.

Citrus syrup

Juice the orange and the lemon into a pan with the sugar and bring all ingredients to the boil, then remove the pot from the heat and leave the syrup to cool.

Glazing

Carefully turn the cake out of the tin and place it on a tray. While the cake is still warm, use a pastry brush to gently distribute the citrus syrup onto all sides of the cake, making sure all the syrup is absorbed into the cake.

PEPPARKAKOR

Makes 10 cookies

7g cinnamon powder
4g clove powder
3g ginger powder
2g nutmeg powder
2g Seville orange peel
40g cream, 38% fat
20g milk, 3.5% fat
60g golden syrup
250g white flour, 11% protein
80g white sugar
1g salt
4g baking soda
60g salted butter, soft

Spread the spices on a baking tray lined with baking paper and toast them in the oven for 2–3 minutes.

Place the cream in a pan and heat to 70°C / 158°F. Remove the pan from the heat, add the toasted spices, and leave the mixture to cool slightly.

Mixing
Place the milk, cream and golden syrup into the bowl of a stand mixer with the paddle attachement. Add the flour, sugar, salt, baking soda and butter and mix until combined.

Preheat the oven to 160°C / 320°F on the convection setting (fan bake). Line a baking tray with baking paper.

Cut out
Using a heavy rolling pin, roll out the dough on a lightly floured surface to 2mm / 0.08in thickness. Punch out the dough using a 10cm / 4in cutter or other shapes as desired. Transfer the cookies to the tray lined with baking paper. Any excess dough can be kneaded back together and re-rolled out several times.

Baking
Place the cookies into the oven on the middle rack and bake for 7 minutes, then turn the tray to ensure even baking and bake for a further 5–6 minutes. It is important that the cookies are baked till fully crisp.

ORANGE CONFIT

Makes about 30 pieces

2 oranges
125g water
125g white sugar
125g glucose

Chocolate tempering
200g dark chocolate, 70% cacao

Day 1
Cut the oranges into quarters. Peel the skin away from the flesh (keep the flesh for juice). Cut the orange peel into quarters.

In a large pot, bring water to a boil. Blanch the orange peel in the boiling water, then transfer to ice water to remove the bitterness. We recommend blanching at least 4 times, and possibly more if the orange peel remains bitter.

After blanching, drain the peel and arrange each piece on a wire rack. Leave it in a warm, dry place and allow to dry for 1 day or so.

Day 2
Bring to boil the water, sugar and glucose. Once boiling, add the pieces of orange peel and bring to a simmer. Simmer the peels for 2 hours 45 minutes, until they are translucent and easy to cut through. Take the pieces out of the confit and lay them individually on a tray lined with baking paper. Leave them to slightly dry until they are no longer sticky to the touch.

Temper the chocolate (see page 336).

Dip half of each orange confit in tempered dark chocolate and arrange on a fresh piece of baking paper. Leave them to set for 1 hour.

FRENCH NOUGAT

Makes 12 pieces

150g Valencia almonds
200g honey
90g water
30g glucose
315g white sugar
35g egg whites

Chocolate
200g tempered chocolate (page 336)

Preparation
Preheat oven to 150°C / 302°F. Spread the almonds on a baking tray lined with baking paper and place them in the oven, checking every 3–4 minutes until evenly roasted.

Scale the honey into a steel pot. Heat until it reaches 121°C / 250°F and maintain this temperature.

In a second pot, scale the water, glucose and 300g sugar. Place the egg whites and 15g of sugar in the bowl of a stand mixer with the whisk attachment and whisk on low speed. Gradually add the honey to the egg whites. Then increase the speed of the mixer to medium.

While the egg whites and honey are mixing, bring the water, glucose and sugar to 142°C / 288°F. Then pour the mixture in a steady stream into the egg white mixture and continue to whisk for 3–4 minutes on medium speed.

Exchange the whisk attachment to the paddle attachment and beat for a further 2–3 minutes. Add the almonds to the mixture and beat until fully coated.

Place the mass between two pieces of baking paper and, using a rolling pin, gently roll it out until about 2cm / 0.8in thick. Leave to rest for 4 hours at room temperature.

Take the mass out of the fridge and cut it into 10 by 2cm / 4 × 0.8in rectangles.

Chocolate coating
Follow the chocolate tempering guide (page 336). Dip one piece at a time into the tempered chocolate, completely enveloping each individual part. Transfer the pieces to baking paper.

Allow them to set for 20 minutes before serving.

ROCHER

Makes 30 pieces (about 350g)

Caramelised almond sticks
40g almond sticks
10g odourless sunflower oil
18g icing sugar
2g vanilla sugar

Rocher mix
75g dark milk chocolate, 40% cocoa
75g Gianduja, 35% hazelnut
110g hazelnut praline paste
35g caramelised almond sticks, chopped
Pinch of sea salt

Chocolate for covering
200g dark chocolate, 60% cocoa, tempered

Preparation
Preheat the oven to 150°C / 302°F on convection setting and line a baking tray with baking paper.

Caramelised almond sticks
Place the almond sticks on the baking tray and toast them in the oven, checking every 3–4 minutes until lightly and evenly toasted. Remove the sticks from the oven and allow them to cool.

The following process will produce a fair amount of smoke, so please make sure that your extraction fan is on the highest setting.

In a large pot with a heavy base, warm up the sunflower oil on medium heat. In two separate containers, scale the icing sugar and vanilla sugar. Add the toasted almond sticks to the pot, roll them around to warm up evenly. A large metal spoon works well for this. When the almond sticks are hot, add half of the icing sugar. Roll the almond sticks in the icing sugar, stirring constantly. Add the remaining half of the icing sugar while stirring. The almond sticks need to be completely coated and caramelised in the sugar. Once the caramelisation is done, turn off the heat and add in the vanilla sugar while stirring. Transfer the caramelised sticks to a tray lined with baking paper and allow them to cool.

Scale and set aside about 50g of the almond sticks, these will be used for topping the rocher. Chop the remaining almond sticks into roughly 5mm / 0.2in pieces.

Rocher mix
Line a baking tray, 11cm × 11cm and 2.5cm deep / 4.4 × 4.4 × 1in, with baking paper. This tray will act as the mould for the rocher mixture.

Melt the dark milk chocolate in a large pot on low heat. Chop the Gianduja block and use a microwave or double boiler to melt it down.

In a large mixing bowl, mix together the chocolate and the Gianduja with the praline paste. Fold in the chopped almond sticks and a pinch of sea salt. Pour the mixture into the lined baking tray and place 50g of the un-chopped almond sticks on top of the mixture in an even layer. Store in the fridge for at least 2 hours till set.

→

Dividing
Check the rocher mixture. It needs to be completely firm and set before dividing. If not there yet, return it to the fridge and check again after 30 minutes.

Turn the set rocher mixture out of the tray and onto a cutting board. Using a ruler, measure out the mass into 2cm / 0.8in squares. Using a large sharp chef's knife, cut the mass into 2cm / 0.8in cubes.

Chocolate coating
Line a tray that can be put in the fridge with baking paper. Temper 200g of 60% dark chocolate (see tempering guide, page 336).

When the chocolate is ready, coat the cubes one by one. Use a sharp mini-skewer to poke into the cube and transfer it into the chocolate. Coat the cube completely and place it onto the tray with baking paper. Continue with the remaining cubes of rocher. Place the tray in the fridge until the chocolate is set.

MENDIANTS

Makes 12–16 pieces

100g dark chocolate, 70% cacao

Toppings
20g dried cherries
20g orange confit (page 288), chopped (1cm / 0.4in)
20g dried cranberries
20g hazelnuts, roasted and peeled
20g green pistachios

Preparation
Organize the toppings so they are easy to access. Prepare a baking tray that fits into your fridge with baking paper.

Temper the chocolate (see page 336) and transfer it to a piping bag.

Pipe 12–16 rounds, about 6–8g each, of tempered chocolate onto the baking paper. Place a few pieces of the different toppings onto each round of chocolate, creating your own mix of fruits and nuts.

Store in the fridge for 4 minutes until the chocolate is set. Remove the tray from the fridge and leave the mendiants at room temperature for 30 minutes before serving.

KRANSEKAGE

Makes 18 pieces

500g marzipan, 66% Valencia almond, 34% sugar
150g white sugar
½ lemon
½ orange
½ tonka bean, grated
35g egg whites
4g rum

Decoration icing
40g icing sugar
8g egg whites, pasteurized

Chocolate base
200g dark chocolate, 70% cocoa

Preheat the oven to 180°C / 356°F on the top and bottom heat setting. Line a baking tray with baking paper.

Preparation
Zest the orange and lemon and grate the tonka bean.

Mixing
In the bowl of a stand mixer with paddle attachment, mix marzipan, sugar, lemon zest, orange zest and grated tonka bean at slow speed. Gradually add the egg whites and rum and mix until smooth and combined.

Scale the mixture into pieces of about 35g. Using two spoons, shape each piece into a quenelle and place them on the lined baking tray.

Bake the cakes for 12 minutes, turn the baking tray around and bake for a further 6–8 minutes or until the top edges are light-golden brown. The centre should be set but still moist when cooled.

Decoration
In a metal mixing bowl, whisk together the icing sugar and egg whites till completely smooth. Transfer to a piping bag. When the kransekage is completely cool, pipe different patterns of the icing onto the surface to give them your own signature.

Chocolate base
Following the chocolate tempering guide (page 336), temper the chocolate. Prepare a tray with a fresh sheet of baking paper. Dip the bottom 3–4mm / 0.2in (lengthwise) of each piece into the chocolate and transfer them to the baking paper.

Allow the pieces to set for 10–15 minutes before serving.

RONDO
Thise

CHEESE

BMO
GOUGÈRES
COMTÉ AND POPPYSEED STICKS

We first met Christophe in his cheese shop, La Fromagerie, just a block away from the bakery, while searching for a supplier of cheese a few months before opening. Having recently returned from living in Paris, we were desperate for good French cheese. In Paris, Nina and I had been lucky enough to live just down the road from Barthélémy, which, to us, is one of the best cheese shops in the world and so had for years been able to indulge in aged Comté from the producer Marcel Petite. Christophe quickly agreed that the aged Comté from Marcel Petite was the very best, and this marked the beginning of our long friendship. We use it mostly for our BMO – or, as it translates: bread with cheese, a breakfast staple in Denmark. The nutty umami character of the aged Comté is a perfect match for our sourdough rolls with a generous layer of salted butter. The gougères and poppyseed sticks are also scrumptious snacks for any occasion.

52
KODAK PORTRA 800-2
53
KODAK
M ---- 1/180
AEOver A
617
M ---- 1/180
AEOver A
618

RA 800-2
54
KODAK
PORTRA 800-2
1/180
619
1/180
620

BMO

Makes 2 rolls with butter and cheese

2 sourdough rolls (page 54)
30g salted butter, room temperature
8 slices Comté cheese

Slice the sourdough rolls in half and generously butter both sides. Finish with four slices of freshly sliced Comté.

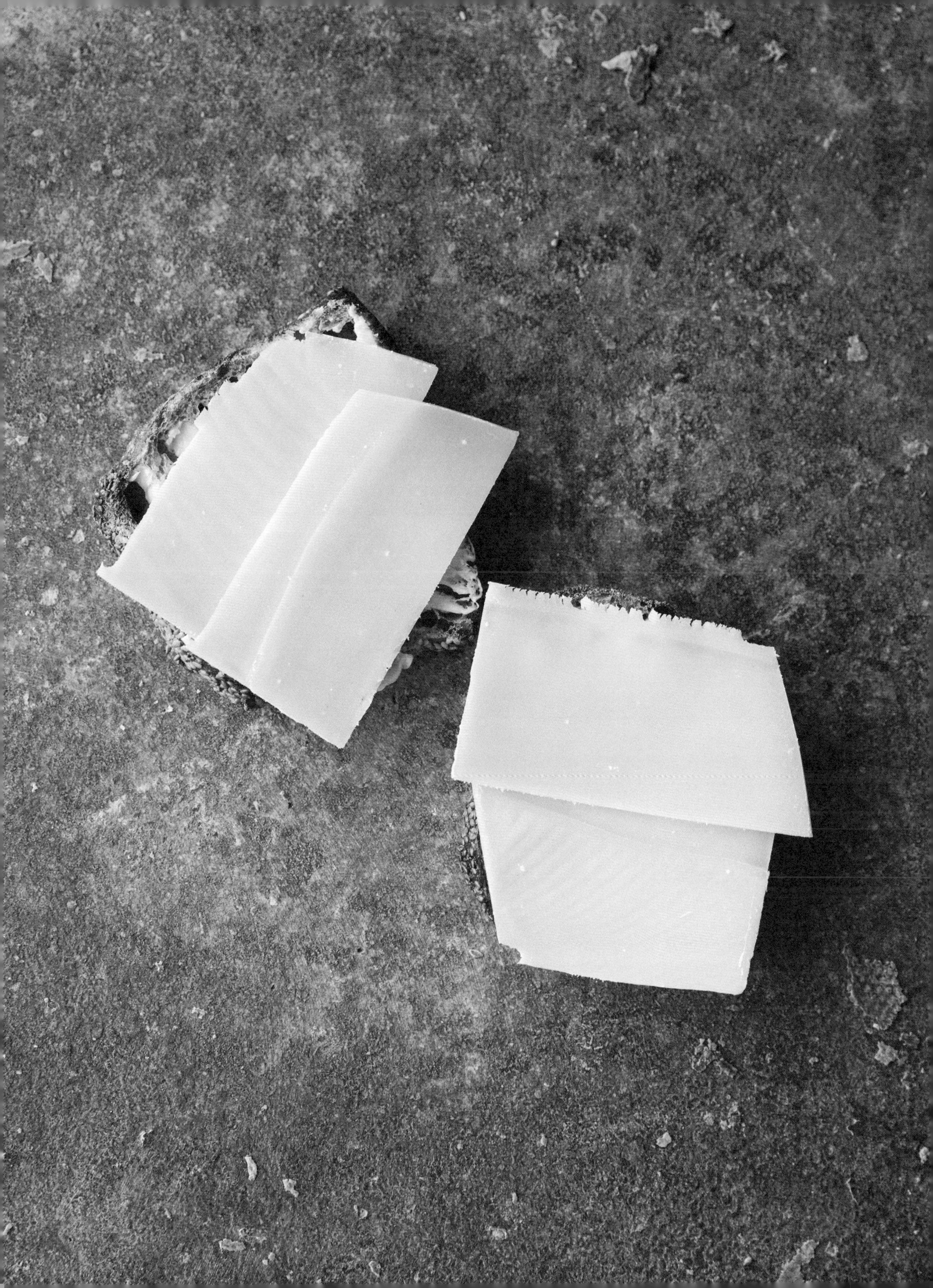

GOUGÈRES

Makes about 20 pieces

35g water
95g milk, 3.5% fat
2 pinches of salt
75g salted butter
115g white flour, 11% protein
75g Comté cheese, grated
2.5 medium to large eggs

Egg wash
2 whole eggs

In a pot, bring the water, milk, salt and butter to a boil. Add the flour and cook it well on low to medium heat, whisking constantly for 4–5 minutes. Transfer the mixture into the bowl of a stand mixer with paddle attachment. Add the grated Comté and mix on slow speed until combined. When the mixture has cooled down slightly, continue mixing and add the eggs one at a time. Mix just until fully combined.

Transfer the mixture to an airtight container and store in the fridge overnight.

Shaping and baking
Preheat the oven to 160°C / 320°F on top and bottom heat setting. Line a large baking tray with baking paper.

Whisk the eggs for the egg wash and prepare a pastry brush.

Remove the mixture from the fridge and scale the dough into 20g pieces. Ball them between your hands until round. Place the balls on the tray evenly spaced apart, leaving 3–4cm / 1.5–2in between. Then carefully brush each piece with egg wash.

Put tray in the oven on the middle rack. Bake the balls for 20 minutes. Turn the tray to ensure even baking. Check and bake for 5 minutes more until the balls are golden brown.

COMTÉ AND POPPYSEED STICKS

Makes 14–15 pieces

Croissant dough (page 82)
1 block of rested laminated croissant dough

Cheese
100g Comté cheese

Poppyseeds
50g white poppyseeds
50g black poppyseeds

Egg wash
2 eggs, beaten

Remove the rested laminated dough from the fridge and begin rolling it out to approximately 3.5mm thick, 30cm high, 36cm long / 0.14 × 12 × 14.2in.

Divide the dough into 2 pieces down the centre, horizontally, making two rectangles 15cm high, 36cm long / 6 × 14.2in. Place a ruler along the base of each rectangle and make markings at 2cm / 0.8in increments. Repeat at the top. Using a sharp knife, cut vertical lines from the top markings to the bottom. Place your strips on a tray and wrap it tightly in cling film. Rest them in the fridge for 10 minutes to cool.

Poppyseed mix
Mix the poppyseeds together in a wide container.

Shaping
Remove the strips from the fridge. In the centre of each piece make a 13cm / 5in cut, leaving 1cm / 0.4in attached at the top and bottom. Pick up the dough by the top and bottom. Keep your left hand still and use your right hand to twist the bottom into the cut centre of the piece. Repeat 3 or 4 times until desired twists are achieved.

After twisting, egg wash the top surface, carefully place it into the poppyseeds and coat completely. Transfer to a tray lined with baking paper, wrap in plastic and store in the fridge. Alternatively, they can be proved and baked on the same day.

Prepare a baking sheet lined with baking paper and tray out the cheese sticks, leaving 3cm / 1.2in between each piece.

Place them into a warm humid place at 28°C / 82°F and prove for about 2 hours until the layers of the sides begin to separate and the volume has increased by 30–40% (see proving advice, page 32).

After about 1.5 hours, preheat the oven to 200°C / 392°F on the convection setting.

When fully proved, place the tray with the sticks on the middle rack of the oven. Bake for 10 minutes, carefully turn the tray to ensure even baking and continue baking for another 2–3 minutes, until golden brown.

Remove the tray from the oven and finely grate a generous amount of Comté over each piece. Place the tray in the oven and bake for another 2 minutes.

FOUNDATION

BUTTER FILLING
SCALD
VANILLA SYRUP
TONKA AND CITRUS SYRUP
ROSE SYRUP
CRÈME PÂTISSIÈRE
DIPLOMAT CREAM
ALMOND OR PISTACHIO FILLING
SABLÉ
PISTACHIO OR HAZELNUT FRANGIPANE
CHOCOLATE TEMPERING

HE

BUTTER FILLING

Makes about 460g

290g salted butter, 12°C / 54°F
190g white sugar
3g fine sea salt

Cut the butter into small cubes in the bowl of a stand mixer. Scale the sugar and salt into the bowl. Mix butter, sugar and salt together at slow speed until just combined (2 minutes). Check that the mixture is evenly combined and if needed mix another 1 minute at slow speed. It's important to avoid over-mixing. Transfer the filling to a microwave-safe plastic or glass container.

SCALD

Makes about 600g

200g white flour, 11% protein
400g boiling water

Mixing
Scale the flour and water. Bring the water to a rolling boil. Pour the water into the base of a stand mixer and immediately add the flour. Mix for 10 minutes at second speed until completely smooth and the starch is fully gelatinised. Alternatively, a hand whisk can be used to blend the scald. It is important to ensure there are no lumps of flour remaining.

Using a pastry scraper, transfer the scald to a sealable heat-safe container and cover the surface completely with cling film. Allow it to cool, then store it in the fridge until used for mixing.

The scald can be kept for 2–3 days in the fridge.

VANILLA SYRUP

Makes about 350g

175g water
10g glucose
150g white sugar
20g vanilla seeds (about 3 large pods scraped out) or 6–7 used vanilla pods

Bring the water, glucose and white sugar to a boil. Cool slightly and pour the syrup over the vanilla pods. Allow to infuse for at least 24 hours.

The syrup can be stored in the fridge or a cool place out of direct sunlight.

TONKA AND CITRUS SYRUP

Makes about 200g

100g water
100g white sugar
2 tonka beans
Zest of 2 oranges
Zest of 2 lemons
8g dark rum

Using a peeler, remove the orange and lemon zest in large ribbons.

Bring the water and sugar to a boil, add the orange and lemon zest and the tonka beans. Remove the pot from the heat, briefly allow the syrup to cool and mix in the rum. Transfer the syrup to a sealable container and store it in the fridge, leaving the zest and tonka in the syrup to infuse for at least 24 hours.

ROSE SYRUP

Makes about 200g

100g water
100g white sugar
4g rose petal powder
4 drops rose extract

Bring the water and sugar to a boil and add the rose petal powder. Remove the pot from the heat and add the rose extract. Allow to cool and infuse. Once cool, pass the syrup through a fine mesh fabric sieve to remove the rose petal powder.

Reserve the syrup in the fridge until use.

CRÈME PÂTISSIÈRE

Makes 700g, adjust as needed

500g milk, 3.5% fat
½ vanilla pod, scraped
125g egg yolks
70g white sugar
40g corn starch
25g salted butter

In a heavy-bottomed stainless steel pot, bring the milk and the vanilla to the boil. In a large steel bowl, whisk together the egg yolks, sugar and corn starch until smooth. Once the milk has reached boiling, pour one third into the egg yolk mixture. Whisk gently to temper the egg yolks, then add the rest of the milk while whisking. Transfer back into the pot and cook out until it starts to thicken, then proceed to cook out for a further 2 minutes over medium heat. Be careful that the base of the pot doesn't overheat.

Remove the pot from the heat and whisk in the butter. Transfer to a heat-proof container with a lid, cover the surface with cling film to prevent skin from forming.

Place into the fridge to set overnight, or at least 3–4 hours.

DIPLOMAT CREAM

Makes 500g

250g cream, 38% fat
250g crème pâtissière (page 326)

In the bowl of a stand mixer, whip the cream on medium to high speed, till soft peaks. Mix the crème pâtissière in a mixing bowl with a whisk until smooth. Gently fold the whipped cream into the crème pâtissière.

Place it into piping bags and store it in the fridge.

ALMOND OR PISTACHIO FILLING

Makes 800g

290g extra fine almond flour or finely ground green pistachio kernels
240g white sugar
25g white flour, 11% protein
8g fine sea salt
12g rum
85g egg whites, pasteurised
90g salted butter
65g glucose

If preparing pistachio filling, start by grinding the pistachios in a food processor until a coarse flour is formed.

Scale the dry ingredients into the bowl of a stand mixer and mix together until combined. Scale the rum and egg whites together into another bowl. Warm the butter in a pot until soft. Heat the glucose in the microwave until it pours easily. Add the soft butter to the dry ingredients and mix until combined. Pour ribbons of glucose into the mixing bowl and mix until combined. Finally add the rum and egg whites and mix until combined.

Transfer the filling to a container with a lid and store it in the fridge until ready to use.

SABLÉ

Makes enough for 10 tart shells

260g white flour, 11% protein
130g icing sugar
25g super fine-ground almonds
2g salt
175g salted butter, soft
25g glucose
50g egg yolks

Mixing
Sieve the dry ingredients into the bowl of a stand mixer using the paddle attachment and mix until combined. Add the softened butter and mix till a crumbly consistency. Add the glucose and the egg yolks gradually while on a low speed. Mix until the sablé is combined and homogeneous.

Place the sablé onto a floured table top and knead to get rid of any residual lumps. Wrap the dough in cling film and let it rest in the fridge for at least 2 hours.

Once rested, place the dough on a floured tabletop and, using a rolling pin, roll it out into a rectangle 2mm / 0.08in thick. Using a docking tool roll over the whole sheet of sablé. Alternatively, a fork can be used to prevent uneven rising. Punch out the dough, using a 10cm / 4in ring cutter, and place the discs in the fridge to rest for 20 minutes.

In the meantime, grease ten 8cm / 3in tart tins.

Tart lining
Take the pre-cut discs from the fridge, warming each disc slightly with the heat from your hands to make the dough pliable. Using the pads of your thumbs, gently push the dough into the edges of the tart tins, ensuring no air pockets are formed in the process. Place the tins in the fridge and chill once again for 20 minutes until the dough hardens. Take the tins out of the fridge and trim the edges to get rid of any excess dough.

If not used right away, the tart shells should be reserved in the fridge.

PISTACHIO OR HAZELNUT FRANGIPANE

Makes about 550g

125g ground hazelnut or pistachio kernels
125g white sugar
1g salt
125g salted butter, soft
125g eggs
38g white flour, 11% protein

For both the hazelnut and pistachio variations of this frangipane, put the nuts in a food processor and grind till a coarse, flour-like consistency.

Put the sugar, salt and ground nuts in the mixing bowl of a stand mixer with the paddle attachment. Add about a third of the soft butter at a time while mixing at slow speed, scrape down the sides of the mixing bowl after each addition of butter. There is no need to aerate the mixture. Once the butter is fully combined, start adding the eggs one by one and the flour in small portions. Once homogeneous, scrape down the bowl to make sure all the ingredients are well incorporated and mix briefly till combined.

Transfer the frangipane to a piping bag. For our 8cm / 3in fruit tarts about 35g of frangipane is normally used.

CHOCOLATE TEMPERING

500g dark chocolate, 60% cacao

For the recipes in the book, the simplest method of chocolate tempering will work well. We recommend selecting the highest quality chocolate possible and following the instructions of your chocolate producer in regard to the exact temperatures for that chocolate. The temperatures stated in the guide are specific to the 60% dark chocolate that we use for our products. Please adapt as necessary to suit the chocolate. It is recommended to temper around 500g of chocolate, as it can be extra challenging to manage the temperature fluctuations with smaller amounts. The extra chocolate can always be saved and reused.

Set up a bain-marie (double boiler) by placing a pot on the stove with a few centimetres of water. Place a metal mixing bowl on top of the pot, so that it is heated by the steam from the water. The bottom of the bowl should not be touching the water.

Chop the chocolate into small pieces and, in a metal mixing bowl over a bain-marie, melt the chocolate until 47°C / 117°F and completely melted, stir continuously with a silicone spatula. When the temperature is reached, remove the bowl from the pot. Continue stirring and cool the chocolate to 27°C / 81°F. Ensure that the chocolate is well combined so that the temperature is even. Return the chocolate to the bain-marie and warm the chocolate up while stirring, until 29°C / 84°F all through.

The chocolate is now ready to use for dipping and coating. Depending on the room temperature, the chocolate will only remain liquid enough for coating for a short period of time. If your room temperature is very low, it can be helpful to fill a pot with lukewarm water, around 29°C / 84°F, and place the chocolate bowl on top; the water should not touch the base of the bowl. This will extend the time that the chocolate will stay well-tempered.

If the chocolate becomes too cool, repeat the steps above and re-temper it. The chocolate can always be cooled and tempered again if needed.

JUNO the bakery

INDEX

Juno the Bakery
– Crafted in Copenhagen

Editing: Hanne Rask
Project management: Louise Haslund-Christensen
Editorial assistance: Anna Birkegaard Raackmann
Thuesen and Caroline Lunde Guldager-Nielsen
Copyediting: Cornelius Holck Colding
Photos: Petra Kleis
Layout: Spine Studio
Typeset in: Medium LL
Paper: 130 Munken Polar
Image processing: Petra Kleis
Printing and binding: Livonia Print

Printed in EU 2026
1st edition, 2nd printing

ISBN 978-87-94418-64-5

Strandberg Publishing
Klareboderne 3
1115 Copenhagen K
mail@strandbergpublishing.dk
www.strandbergpublishing.dk

Part of the Gyldendal Group